"The Voyage of the Norman D." is as amazing a creation in realism for a twelve years' child as "The House Without Windows" was amazing in fantasy for a nine years'. I see the same gifts, however, in each: the child's zest for living, changing normally from fantasy to realism in just those years, the wholly extraordinary thing being the degree and the coherence of that zest, the completeness of the child's absorption in the experience and the completeness of the absorption of the experience by the child. But the call of life is so healthy; there is none of the hectic and exotic of the "prodigy" in her living, apparently. And her writing has nothing of the child's imitation: it is complete, zestful transmutation of her child's experience into amazingly effective language — and, as such, is as much art as any grown up's transmutation.

— William Ellery Leonard, Department of English, University of Wisconsin

It is wise that the age of the author of this book (thirteen years) should be explained on the jacket. Otherwise, so simple a response to beauty as the writing displays would announce a talent which could find no comfortable place in a literary world rotten with cheap sophistication, where nothing is so desirable as an epigrammatic cliché and nothing so troublesome as untutored sentiment. Barbara Follett took a trip to Nova Scotia on a lumber schooner. What the crew thought of it we can't imagine. But what she thought of it is a delight to read. It was beautiful and strange. Her imagination leapt to meet the old ways of skies, ships, and sailors, and the deep excitement of the sea. The occasional self-consciousness of the writing only serves to endear the young author by making her so evidently a real child of thirteen.

— Frances Lamont Robbins, *Spring Reading*, The Outlook (New York)

This is a most improbable sort of book, yet when read it becomes utterly convincing. The impression one gathers is that Barbara, who has never been to school, is that rare being, a completely normal and intelligent child. She had a passion for ships and the sea. She dredged the dictionary for the meanings of every nautical term she had ever heard of. She dragged her family down to the river at New Haven to look at a lumber schooner and promptly began to climb the rigging. She seems to be endowed with an almost miraculous faculty for making friends with strangers and managing her family. She surmounted unbelievable obstacles in the way of a thirteen-year-old girl shipping for a voyage to Canada and she narrates the whole thing with a gusto, a vividness and with what the jacket-blurb calls (with perfect justness) "such a fervor of devotion" that the grown-up reader simply falls head-over-heels in love with Barbara and swallows every word she says.

— William McFee, *A Most Piratical Maiden,* New York Herald Tribune Books

When "The House Without Windows," that amazing monument to the intensity of a child's inner life first appeared, one was left wondering just what direction the young author's next adventure would take. "The Voyage of the Norman D." seems at first glance as unlike the story of Eepersip as could well be imagined, but in reading it one recognizes more and more strongly the logical development. In Eepersip the experience took place largely in the mind; here it is in every day life, but the spirit that made the imaginary adventure real lifts the actual one, in turn, into the region of vision and mystery. The book is the account of a trip taken by the thirteen-year-old author on a lumber schooner bound for Canada, working as cabin-boy, and living the life of the crew. I mention age only because it happens to be mentioned in the preface, since art has in itself nothing to do with years. "The Voyage of the Norman D." is a fine, sustained, and vivid piece of writing that would do credit to a writer of my age, and I very much doubt whether an older mind would have got so much out of the experience or brought nearly so much to the writing of it.

— Margery Williams Bianco, *New Horizons*, Saturday Review of Literature

At fourteen years of age, Barbara Newhall Follett, the girl born with "the piratical tendency," has narrated her adventures in a vivid, unaffected book called "The Voyage of the Norman D." Going out as a cabin boy on a schooner among rough seamen, holding her own in the hard work, sharing the dangers of climbing the rigging in nasty weather, she has much to her credit. It is an infant female Roosevelt we have here.

— *In Brief Review*, The Bookman

It is a fascinating book from several points of view; chiefly, I think, because it is a good piece of writing apart from any consideration of the author's age. Barbara shows the same delight in natural beauty which came out so strongly in her "House Without Windows," but she expresses it more easily and more maturely. Her sense of form, of the dramatic suspense of a story, has grown, and her feeling for the drama and humor of character has developed... Barbara Follett has a distinct writing bent, an inherent ability to express herself in words and an inherent love of doing it.

— Helen Hammett Owen, *Sailing a Ship*, New York Herald Tribune Books

The Voyage of the Norman D.

as told by the cabin-boy

Barbara Newhall Follett

farksolia

First published in the United States of America by Alfred A. Knopf, 1928

Farksolia edition © 2024 Barbara Newhall Follett & Stefan William Follett Cooke

All rights reserved.

No part of this book may be reproduced in any form or by any electronic or mechanical means, including information storage and retrieval systems, without written permission from the author, except for the use of brief quotations in a book review.

Cover design by Resa Blatman • resablatman.com

For more BNF, please visit farksolia.org

ISBN: 978-0-9962431-7-9 (softcover)

Note from the Publisher

The manuscript from which this book is set is the carbon copy of a letter which the author wrote, during the weeks just following her return from the voyage recorded, to a distant friend with whom (as appears in the context) she had long had some piratical understandings. She mailed it in eight-page typewritten installments as they were produced. The book is identical with the letter except in the following particulars: (1) Many purely personal passages are omitted. (2) Much repetition due to the haste of first composition has been weeded out. (3) The name of the actual schooner and the names of some of the crew have been disguised. (4) The division into sections is an afterthought. (5) The endpapers consist of a document in code with which the author amused herself during one interval in the composition of the letter.

 The narrative represents chiefly two obvious traits of its author. The first is a circumstantial memory. (Her jottings made day by day throughout the voyage, four pages all told, served but to recall changes of weather and stages of progress.) The second is that same intense natural love of natural beauty

Note from the Publisher

which found its first public expression in *The House Without Windows and Eepersip's Life There* (1927). In *The House Without Windows* this passion clothed itself in fantasy which incorporated here and there some details of actual experience. In this record of an actual experience, it clothes itself in a shimmering veil of fantasy, so transparent that the actuality of the basic experience is rather heightened than obscured.

The voyage was taken three months after the author's thirteenth birthday. The book comes to publication a little before her fourteenth. It is, then, the spontaneous output of a very young writer who, as it happens, has never as yet had a day of formal schooling, and who learns her craft by that simplest of all processes, enjoying with abandon whatever comes into her life, reading with absorption whatever comes into her hands, and writing with demoniacal energy whatever comes into her head. To the publisher, it seems that this one exhibit justifies her obvious contentment with the schooling which, for part of an ecstatic month, was got out of the *Norman D.*, her rigging and sails and crosstrees, the men of her cabin and her forecastle; and out of the various magic of the waters beneath her keel.

Note from the New Publisher

The above Note was included in Alfred A. Knopf's edition of *The Voyage of the Norman D.,* which was published in May 1928. Regarding item (4) in the first paragraph, I've removed Knopf's distracting "sections," which were brief descriptions printed at the top of each righthand page such as "Nautical Fare," "Words on the Weather," and "Disrespectful." As for item (5), I've included Barbara's document in code near the end of this book.

I've also added a new Afterword, which attempts to

Note from the Publisher

describe Barbara's life shortly before and following her voyage on the *Frederick H.* (the *Norman D.*'s true identity).

Lastly, I've included Wilson Follett's *Notes on a Junior Author (with a glance at precocity)*, which was commissioned by *The Horn Book* and published to coincide with *The Voyage of the Norman D.* It appeared in the May 1928 issue. My grandfather died about a month after I was born and almost everything I know about him comes from his novel (*No More Sea*), short stories, essays, and letters to family members. I'm not happy with the ways he treated his three families, particularly in his wife Helen's and daughters Barbara's and Sabra's cases, but I find much to agree with in *Notes on a Junior Author*. What he has to say about Barbara's maturity or lack thereof is fascinating to me, as is his description of his daughter's education, which took place mainly out of doors and far from the influence of the dreaded "educational psychologists."

The Cottage in the Woods
Lake Sunapee, New Hampshire
July 23, 1927

DEAR ALAN:

Thank you a lot for your very mysterious letter from Honolulu. I wish I could have been with you. But the Congressmen and their families must have been a bore. I could have helped you concoct a regular mutiny, and, with me aboard, you may be sure it would have been done in a piratical way. I should have accosted the desperate-looking sailor and become acquainted with him. That would have been the first step.

Well, I feel tempted to sail full force into my own adventures, even if they are not so exciting and mysterious as your own. For the adventures that have befallen me since you set sail for Sulu are wilder and rasher than anything you ever heard me tell you before.

You know very well (better than anyone, I think) my profound devotion to pirates and things piratical. And you know, too, about the pirate tales which I started a little while before you went away — very bloody, exciting, villainous, profane stories, were they not? I had such a great many ideas for pirate stories (and more and more ideas kept showing their faces), I finally decided that my pirates would make a much greater showing if I blended all the short tales I had written, and a great many more that I had in my mind, into one moderately long story. No sooner said than I started to work.

I found, in the course of the very first few pages, that I was getting involved in considerable difficulties. There had to be ships, that was certain; but I found that I knew almost nothing about ships. So I laid the story aside a little while, turned to

Webster, and buried my face in the dictionary. I looked up every nautical term that I could think of, whether I knew it or not. I looked up nautical words found in books I had read. I studied the list of nautical words and their meanings at the end of *The Dauber*. Then the sails bothered me. I needed to know something about sails, and about different kinds of rigs, and about the fastenings of the sails and the names of them all. So I turned to the word sail, and — lo and behold! exactly what I wanted. Accompanying the word *sail* were two pictures, one of the schooner or fore-and-aft rig, and the other of the beautiful square-rig, each sail numbered and named below. I fell to work with great zeal, and learned topsails, topgallants, royals, skysails, jibs, staysails, and all the rest of them; I can reel them off now like second nature.

Then I realized that I didn't know much about rigging and ropes — the uses, the names of them. I found just what I wanted under the word *ship*. It was a picture of a ship in diagram, showing all the principal ropes, spars, and yards. There were close to two hundred figures in all, but I settled right down to business and learned just about everything: lifts, braces, clews, stays, backstays, sheets, ratlines, tops, caps — the whole works. I don't know how many exciting hours I spent at my dictionary, digging into a perfect treasure-trove of nautical words. I never in my life before realized how many nautical terms there are. And I was getting very gay indeed. I was really learning something, and I was not slow to make use of my knowledge. I danced around the house, shouting out ship words and phrases which I had found in *Treasure Island* and other books, but which now had a new meaning for me. The first result was that my pirate story gradually began to improve a great deal. The second result was far more important.

I found myself going about to various people to find out still more about ships. But I based most upon the dictionary; I was sure that was correct, at any rate. I found myself getting crazy and crazier about ships (whether pirate ships or not — though of course they were preferable), and about the sea. I found that *my own writing* was getting me into a wild state. My own writing was making me want to sail. Now, if somebody else's writing (the writing of somebody who had really sailed) had been making me crazy about it, I should not have been so surprised. But when I had never sailed, and knew nothing about ships except what I had learned from Webster's Dictionary — that seemed strange indeed. Whether from one source or another, *something* made me want to sail, and so badly that my blood fairly itched within me, and I went after the dictionary harder than ever, in case an opportunity should suddenly come up; for I wanted to be well prepared.

This was the second result (or, at least, the beginning of it), and I presume it was making me a bit hard to live with. One day Mother took me over to see old Mr. Rasmussen. Mr. Rasmussen is the chief carpenter of the house they are putting up behind ours, and, so Mother had discovered some time before, he had been a sailor all his life. I had told her very savagely that I had determined to sail. Even a schooner "would do," thought I, though of course a square-rigged ship would do better. Mother tried at first to dissuade me. She told me that the only schooners in existence now, as far as she knew, were the fishing schooners that came into Boston, and they were so soaked with fish and fish oil that they were really quite unbearable. But I was not to be dissuaded so easily, though I did begin to wish that I had been alive in the days of the great old clipper ships, dashing across the Atlantic from England to America. I was furious with myself for living at a time when the beauty and stateliness and romance of sailing ships had dwindled down to a few stenching schooners in Boston Harbor.

* * *

WELL, then, I went over to see Mr. Rasmussen. You would love talking with him, Alan. He is full of tales of his old sailing days, and rattles them off even while he is sawing lumber or driving nails. And as for knowledge, why, ships are second nature to him. The sea is in every line of his face, too. He has a mass of wrinkles radiating from the corners of his eyes, from squinting in the sun and looking off into the dazzling sea. He is brawny, firmly muscled, and tattooed on the inside of his left forearm. He is delightfully disgusted with things on land. I remarked to him, as he was up on the scaffolding: "Well, that kind of rigging isn't so much fun, is it?" He replied instantly: "No, too steady. Hasn't got give enough. (He said "gib.") He has a quaint power of description, too. He tells about typhoons off the China coast — says "you would think a pack of demons was loose on the sea." Mr. Rasmussen, by the way, has a forty-foot sloop of his own, and about every two weeks he goes off in it for the week-end, going over to Block Island to fish. He has promised me that I shall go with him on one of those trips sometime.

But, to go on with the story, Mother said to him: "I've got a daughter here who's gone crazy about boats. We thought you ought to know about all the sailing ships there are, and we wondered if you knew where there is a schooner or square-rigger that is working now."

Says he: "Why, yes, indeed. There's a nice little schooner come in New Haven now; she come in right ahead of me last Monday. She come down with lumber from Nova Scotia. Pretty boat, too — all white. I think her name is *Norman D.*"

"Do you think there's any chance we could go aboard of her, mate?" I asked. (I liked to pretend that he had been a shipmate of mine.)

"Go aboard of her? Oh my, yes — they'd be tickled to death to have a chance to show somebody the boat. The crew are all home boys, and I guess they're mighty lonely down here where they don't know anyone."

He gave us full instructions as to how to get to the schooner, and we resolved to go the next day. I stayed and had a little talk with the old sailor. He says: "I usually go out o' port on Friday. Now, 'tain't commonly supposed to be lucky to leave port on a Friday, but I don't take no stock in superstition. I once sailed along of a captain that wouldn't leave port on a Friday, even when there was good wind, good tide, good weather — everything just right."

* * *

MATE, you can believe that I hardly slept a wink all that night. I was going down to see a real schooner. I was going aboard of her. I should see the crew, and be friendly with them. I should climb up in the rigging, if allowed. (That was a secret hope of mine, and I was almost more excited about that than anything.) I would show the family, and the crew, too, that if I got a chance to go up in those ratlines, I would go!

We must have made quite a sight, the whole Follett family going down the street under royals and skysails, headed straight for the schooner *Norman D.* It seemed an infinitely long way, but we saw the masts of her as soon as we got out of the trolley car, and I know I was like a bucking wild horse all the way down Brewery Street. When I saw those noble topmasts against the blue sky ahead of me, I wanted to run and get there; but Sabra was with us, and we couldn't hurry. I ran a few steps, excitedly snapping my fingers; then I would buck and wait. So we proceeded down towards the old broken-down wharf. As we came nearer and nearer, though not yet near enough to see the white hull of her, the beautiful, stately topmasts and lower masts became clearer and clearer, and at last I could see the rope ladder — the shrouds and ratlines that I might be going up in. And, at the idea of climbing into those spider webs, I was so thrilled that I was almost dizzy, and knew hardly anything.

We came up and up alongside her, till we were right beneath her bulwarks, and saw over us her stately bowsprit, with the jibboom and flying jibboom. I was thrilled to realize that I had already begun to recognize things. I recognized that small vertical spar projecting downward from the jibboom which is called the "dolphin striker." This was one of the many things I had learned from that diagram under the word *ship*.

They were busy discharging her cargo of lumber; the deck load was making good progress. There were three carts on the wharf alongside her, on to which they were loading it. The captain was sitting on the edge of the deckhouse superintending the work, which was going on very briskly. We hailed him: "May we come aboard?"

"Why, I gesso," he replied. "What you want?"

"Oh, we're just landlubbers who want to see your ship."

"Well, come ahead," he said.

So we scrambled over the lumber carts, the whole Follett family, still under full sail and laughing heartily. I was the first upon the bulwarks amidships, and I jumped down and landed with a thump upon the deck load. (Quite a long jump it seemed to me then, but before long I jumped from the bulwarks on to the empty deck without thinking anything of it.)

I spoke to the captain first of all, but very vaguely and dreamily, gazing about me — fascinated, enraptured, all the time. I looked at the long, huge booms, with the sails frapped closely round them; at the great, splendid masts; at the many ropes descending over blocks and made fast on belaying pins along the side of the boat; at the double and triple sheet-blocks;

and, above all, at the ratlines and shrouds, into which I longed to go up. The next minute I had jumped upon the spanker boom and crawled along to the very end, hanging slightly over the water, where I supported myself by one of the wire lifts.

"Oh," said the captain, "I see you're a girl as likes to climb around."

And that was true: for really I liked to climb around even better than I dared admit at first. I climbed many times upon the top of the deckhouse and on to the spanker boom, I walked stealthily and cautiously along the bulwarks, I talked a bit with two of the sailors who were waiting for one of the carts before they began loading again; I laid my hand longingly upon the shrouds. But, though I had plenty of courage, and a lot left over, to climb, I had not quite the courage to ask permission, since I felt sure that I should not be allowed. At last, after I had explored around a bit, after I had taken hold of the vast, hand-worn spokes of the wheel, after I had examined the compass in the binnacle — I went up to the captain and said: "I don't suppose you would let me go up into the rigging, would you?"

"Sure!" he replied, "only stick to the ladder, see? Don't go off the rope ladder — and hold on tight."

"Oh, don't worry," I answered. "I most likely shan't get up very far." And I ran to the starboard mizzen rigging.

There Mother accosted me: "Oh, don't go up there! You scare me to death." I overlooked her entirely, and laid my hand upon the shrouds. Upon the shrouds! I felt a little thrill go through my hand. Next minute I was over the taffrail. "You don't dare, do you?" she continued. "Watch me and see," I replied. Then I pulled up on to the ratlines. The emotions and sensations of that moment are indescribable. I was starting my career as a sailor. I was already in the rigging, and I hadn't been on the ship for more than twenty minutes! And only yesterday, before that talk with my old sailor friend, it was a far-away dream, pretty nearly impossible to accomplish. Things had shaken about strangely. I was in the rigging! Up and up I went, hand over hand. I could have gone much faster without a quiver, but I was so taken by it that I went slowly. I felt the rigging sway beneath my weight. Fascinating! The shrouds were getting closer and closer together, and the ratlines, therefore, shorter and shorter. I was a few steps below the crosstrees. I never believed, never in this world, that I should be able to go more than halfway up. Yet up I went, and the ratlines were so very short that I could just wedge my feet between them. Next moment I had reached out an arm, put it over the crosstrees, braced my foot on the iron futtock shrouds, and pulled myself up. There I was, *sitting on the crosstrees*, one foot braced upon the futtock shrouds, the other foot dangling in midair, sixty-five feet above the deck.

The deck down there looked about six inches long, and the busy crew about the size of ants, yet very clear and sharp. I had never dreamed of being so close to the truck. There was the slender tip of the mizzen-mast hardly twenty feet above me. There I was, sitting on the crosstrees. I thought of many and curious things. It was here that Jim Hawkins had sat, in his terrified flight from Israel Hands. Here I was, and I could imagine an Israel, wounded, dirk in teeth, climbing after me. I stood up on the crosstrees, and, looking out to sea, I found that I could see very far and clearly. A few little harbor boats were cruising about. Yes, the deck was certainly not more than six inches long. But I found, to my intense delight, that I could look down upon it without a tremor. My head is built for height. I have a sailor heart, and a sailor head, thought I. Now, if only I were sure that I had a sailor stomach, everything would be perfect.

It is very alarming to get from the crosstrees on to the ratlines again. It is necessary to hang over space for a moment, until you can get your feet on the rigging. But it did not bother me. I lowered myself by the strength of my forearms, took the futtocks with my hands, and dropped my feet on to the ratlines. Then I came down, feeling, Alan, a good deal more like a real pirate than I had ever felt before.

The captain complimented me gravely, saying: "I couldn't go up as far as that," and telling me that I had a good head.

* * *

THAT was about the end of the first day's climbing. Right now I forget whether I went up again or not, but the first time was the most thrilling, anyway. I talked for a while with two of the sailors; then the captain took us about the ship, showing us the galley, the fo'c'sle, the engine-room, the after cabin. The latter is a very ample, seemingly luxurious place: two moderately large rooms, one used for dining room, which has a massive table hooked up to the wall to prevent its rolling about; the rest of it divided into five small compartments, each containing a bunk. Of these the captain, mate, bo's'n, and cook had four, and the other was a spare bunk. In the fo'c'sle there are bunks for four, but there were only three men there, then. On asking one of the men if that wasn't quite a small crew to handle the schooner, they answered very definitely in the negative.

The captain is a most delightful old fellow, a true sea captain. He will talk for hours at a time. I think he can say as many words in an hour as another man in a day. He told us about various experiences of his in his many schooners — storms, losing deck loads, and so on. He says:

"I'm not boasting, but, folks, I've never lost a ship in my life, and only one deck load. Now, that's a good record for a man that's been at sea forty year. An' I'll tell you, folks, how I lost that deck load. It was in that gale we had last October — on a

Friday, I think 'twas — an' part of the port taffrail got carried away — see there, folks, where you can see that new paint? Well, that's the piece as got carried away, and I see we had to lose that load. So we give it a little start, and, I tell you, folks, it wasn't very hard. All we had to do was give it a little start, and off it went. I had it all insured, folks, and I guess the boys would have been glad enough to have the whole lot go, hold and all! Ha! Ha! Ha!" (It was the same gale that carried down one of the oak trees in the woods near us.)

He evidently liked to boast about his early days at sea. One tale he told which particularly took my fancy: "When I was a greenhorn, I got the hang of a sailor's job pretty quick. I was a smart lad at the helm. The cap'n was particklarly pleased with me. I was proud, I tell you, folks, one time when we was havin' some rough weather. Another greenhorn that put out to sea with me went up aft to take his trick, but he couldn't manage it at all — the waves come breaking over the ship, and the cap'n saw he didn't know the ropes at all. Well, I'd jist had my two hours; I was all through and gone up forrard, but when the cap'n see this lad didn't know nothing, he called me aft agin, and gave me the helm fer another trick. Well, I was proud, I tell you!"

So he rattled on, tale after tale. He was telling us about the schooner he was in command of before the *Norman D.* "She was a sweet schooner, folks," he said; "she would do anything but talk, and she tried hard enough to do that."

For the matter of that, I have said little enough about the *Norman D.* herself. She is a 390-ton schooner. The captain said she used to be 425, but she was cut down, because on a schooner of more than 400 tons, there has to be a certified mate — a mate who has passed examinations and has a license or something of the kind to indicate that he is a competent officer. Nowadays there is so little sailing, and the terms of enlistment are so short, and the men are so unsteady, sailing a few months and then going off ashore somewhere, that they don't get enough training to become certified mates. Therefore mates are very hard to get. So the schooner was cut down. (An ordinary man would have told all that in about three minutes and three quarters, but not so the captain. He told it inside and out, backwards and forwards, two or three times, and we never heard the last of that certified mate.) She has masts of about ninety feet; very fine trees they were once. Her booms are huge, especially the spanker, which is almost as large around as the part of the mast just below the crosstrees. Her jibboom is very long and straight, for she carries an outer jib — jib, flying jib, and outer jib. She is all painted white, with a narrow stripe of red about three feet below the bulwarks, and a little red painted ornament on the top of the cutwater. Her hull seemed to me to be of a beautiful shape — but it was beautiful enough to see a wooden hull at all, these days.

The captain explained to me a great many things about a sailing vessel, and I went home with a much clearer idea of things. He told me all the names of the sails, showed me the gaffs, which I had never quite understood, and told me which sails were usually taken in first in a wind, and which were first hoisted. Like Jim Hawkins when he found Long John Silver, I began to realize that *here* was a *shipmate*! If I could live with Captain Avery for a while, I did not doubt but that I should really know something.

* * *

THERE could be only three or four different results to all this. So far, the result was that we invited the captain out to dinner the next Sunday, and arranged to have the Bryans come over "to meet a real old sea captain." Accordingly, Sunday morning about half-past ten (five bells), I set out alone for the schooner. Again I had the pleasure of seeing her proud and noble topmasts against the sky, but this time I could go tearing at full speed down Brewery Street. Yet I was not so hasty but that I stopped to think a minute. It was Sunday. Very likely the crew would be ashore: suppose there were no one aboard the schooner — no one to let me aboard? Then I should have to go prowling about alone, without permission, sneaking down into the cabin to search out the captain, and I might be suddenly challenged and questioned by one of the sailors. Also it would look rather curious, to anyone ashore, to see me going over the ship's side without permission. I might be in some embarrassing situations before the end of the morning! I confess that I was a little worried, and I stopped tearing along, and walked quietly and decently down the street.

The gate to the wharf was closed, and at that time I didn't know about a certain little side gate, always possible to open by hand. Here was my first barrier. I determined, however, to get to the ship *anyway*; and I pulled lightly over the fence and dropped down upon a heap of coal. Then I started around it. But I was looking down, walking rather fast, and before I saw what I was doing I had brought up short against the bow hawser of the schooner. I was a bit stunned, for the rope was heavy and very taut. I ducked under it and found my way to the side of the schooner.

At first it looked as though the worst of my suspicions were too true. There was not a sign of a soul upon the decks. The whole ship was as still as night. I didn't even hear any voices from the cabin or fo'c'sle. But I determined to stick it out until I knew. The silence was positively terrifying. I could only judge that the captain had gone off to Boston (as he had warned us he might), and that all the rest of the crew were ashore. Yet, I thought, someone ought to be aboard; the ship wouldn't be likely to be left all alone. With this in my mind, I raised a small hail — "Yoo-hoo!" — and, to my delight, someone appeared in the door of the fo'c'sle. Two or three others were behind him, looking curious and rather startled.

I put a very bold and saucy face upon the matter. "Look here," said I, "I'm the kid who was here a couple o' days ago, and the captain was coming out to lunch with us today, so I came down to get him. Is he aboard?"

There were many answers to this question. "The captain's ashore." "I think he's gone to Boston." "No, no," from the cook, "the captain's aft. He ain't gone to Boston."

I thought I had better cover up the toploftiness with which I had started, and I was very pleasant and friendly for a bit. Then I said: "May I go aft and find the captain?" "Yes, indeed," they returned. Meanwhile I had slipped rather sure-footedly from the edge of the wharf to the top of the bulwarks, and leaped down upon the deck. (By this time the deck load of lumber was gone.) I found my way down into the cabin.

Then came the most exciting thing of all, my hunt for Captain Avery. He was not in the dining room or in the other part of the after cabin, where there were a desk and a barometer, a couch and a few chairs. Then I began ransacking the various sleeping compartments — for I did not remember which the captain had said was his. I found him in the second, lying down, fast asleep, his white hair falling over his face, his cheeks rosy, and part of his Sunday clothes on. I waited ten full minutes, I am sure, to see if he wouldn't wake up of his own accord; for if there is anything I detest, it is waking up sleeping persons. At last I said very softly: "Captain Avery!" No answer. Then I tapped gently on the open door, and said again: "Captain Avery!" He woke as though eight bells had struck, or as though the bo's'n had suddenly called "All hands on deck!" And, believe me, there was no yawning or coughing or blinking or rubbing. He was wide awake in a flash — which shows what a sailor he is. He recognized me immediately with a smile. "Well, I guess I dozed off all right. I took it into my head to read, 'n' so I got out my Bible and read a chapter or two. 'N' then I began to feel sleepy, 'n' I jist dozed off." Then he was up and putting the finishing touches to his Sunday dress. I was rather sorry, though, to see the old fellow dressed up. It didn't look right to see him in a stiff collar and a clean white shirt.

He fell to talking immediately, about this and that and the other and why he didn't go to Boston and what the crew was doing and what they wanted to do and what they usually did on Sunday and how they went cruising around and how soon he thought the cargo would be discharged and how long he thought the schooner would be in port — everything all in a jumble, with no commas, just as I have written it. Then he told about his home town, Moncton, Nova Scotia, and the various railway routes and harbors. Also he began to tell what he had done in New Haven, and what a pretty town it was, and how glad he was to have a chance to see more of it, and was I sure about the trolley car routes? and did I have plenty of car-fare? and how far out did we live? and what building was this, and that, and the other? and so on, and so forth, and so following. Then he fell to about ships and schooners; and that I was really glad of, and began to pay more attention. And he began yarning about storms and gales, and furling the sails hastily, and coming through dangerous shoals and shallows under bare poles, until I thought that I had never met such an interesting old codger.

By this time we were in the Whitney Avenue trolley car. The captain was much impressed by the stately elms. They led to a general discussion of all the various trees in all the various parts of the world, especially Nova Scotia. But really the business part of the town was the most interesting to him, and, as I said, he kept asking me about this building and that one till I thought I had never had such a drill on my own home town. All the way up Armory Street he ran on, in a monotone which it often became difficult for me to understand. When we got home I dumped him into a rocking-chair, feeling quite stunned with all the talk I had heard. I was willing to have the air more silent around me, and so I was rather glad when he picked up a newspaper and began to scan it. I never heard anyone so entertaining when reading to himself. He would read the headlines aloud, then the articles to himself, making audible or inaudible comments now and then. And after he had finished he would say: "Hm! And a hard enough time they'll have of it, too!" or the like incomprehensible ejaculation.

All day Sunday he talked in the same way, pouring forth streams of conversation concerning everything under the sun. Of course I liked his ship talk the best, but, since that was second nature to him, he seemed to prefer talking of other things. Late in the afternoon we all went down to take him back to the schooner, and to show her to the Bryans.

I HAVE never managed to go down there without having thrills run through and through me at the sight of the *Norman D.* — her long and graceful jibboom, the sharpness of her white cutwater, her mazes of rigging, ratlines, blocks; even the very idea of her — of a schooner, a real schooner, a large vessel under sails — thrilled me. The bo's'n brought a ladder when he saw the captain coming, and aboard we all went. By this time I had got to feel very much at home on the ship. I wanted to feel at home on her; I loved to, because I felt more than ever like a sailor. I grew, of course, steadily more daring, and now I walked right along the bulwarks without a quiver. The first thing I did when I got aboard was to scramble up the rigging again. Oh, how I loved that rigging! How I loved to grip the shrouds tight, to feel myself going up hand over hand over hand! How I loved the quivering, the shaking, which my weight gave to it! And how I was thrilled, how I was always thrilled, to find myself sitting on the crosstrees!

One thing, however, I had not hitherto dared to venture upon — the topsail ratlines. Just above the crosstrees are five or six more frail rope steps, not nearly so steady and strong as the main part of the rigging. These steps are used when the sailors are aloft working at the topsails. Somehow they looked too frail and shaky for me. I didn't quite dare begin climbing *them*, especially when I was starting more than sixty feet above the deck. But I stood out on the crosstrees, and I put my hand to my forehead, and I looked out to sea — feeling a good deal like the lookout man on the fo'c'sle deck.

By this time they had entirely moved the deck load and were working on the hold (though, of course, not on that day), and so the boom of the mainsail had been belayed to the port side of the schooner, to make room for hoisting out the cargo. Now it was loose, and I had a lot of fun pushing it back and forth. Then I scrambled up on to it — and quite a job that was, too — and Daddy pushed it back and forth, until it swung almost out over the water, bringing up hard on the sheet. Afterwards I learned to get up on the boom in one pull of my arms, by means of the downhaul, but of course the sails weren't hoisted then.

That evening we became acquainted with the mate. He is a very nice fellow. Evidently he had been ashore, for he had on his shore togs. We went up forward on the fo'c'sle deck and had a long talk with him. I happened to hint something about the jibboom. I longed to go out on it, but I didn't quite dare to. I hadn't quite got my sailor-familiarity-with-the-ropes on yet. But the mate immediately started to go out on the bowsprit. "See," said he, "this is a nice, easy little walk out here" — as he went along a shelf of the bowsprit no more than three inches wide, holding on by a wire rope. "See, you just be careful to hold on to this rope — you must be careful to not grab anything that'll let you down." Then he reached the jibboom, and stepped down on to the footropes. "But these footropes are a good long stretch for a youngster," said he. "I tell you, this is a nasty place in bad weather; it certainly is. Imagine how it would be with waves running high, and washing up over you when you are out on there!" Then he told us how once he had managed to fall off the jibboom when a high sea was running, but, happily, had caught by his armpits among the bowsprit rigging and climbed up on again. I surely believed him: I had never known anything, even the topsail ratlines, look more insecure than those footropes. They jerked back and forth, and at every step they sagged 'way down. But I determined to be sailorly, and, though I didn't go out that evening, I secretly resolved that some day I should surprise everyone by going out on those frail, jogging footropes, where, if I should fall off, I should probably stick fast in nice, oozy harbor mud.

HOW that schooner haunted me! I was like a caged lion all day, and at night I dreamed that I was sailing off, back to Nova Scotia, with her. The days were drawing on. She would be going in about two weeks. I should see her no more. Perhaps I should *never* see her again, for Captain Avery has no regular schedule, and he goes into New Haven very rarely. Yes, perhaps I should never see her again. And there would end my brilliantly begun sailor career. Again I should have to resort to the stenching fishing schooners around Boston. The best I could possibly hope for, thought I, would be to go out on the tug which would tow her out of the harbor. Then I could at least see her hoist her sails and sail and roll away. How lonely I should be! I was afraid of the thought. In my imagination I could see her casting her towrope, her sails filling with a fresh breeze, already her cutwater making wings of foam reach out along her sides. I should see her dwindle to a snow-sailed fairy ship in the distance; then she would be a microscopic speck on the horizon. Oh, but that was to die by inches, thought I. I think I could never have borne it.

"Oh! don't you wish we could go with her when she sails?" said I to Daddy, who was fascinated by her, as I was.

"Why yes, of course I do," said he. "But we can't — so there's no use in talking about it."

No, there was certainly no use in talking about it. The impossible cannot be accomplished. But the schooner continued to haunt me.

And so Mother and I escaped from the house and went down to see the schooner again. This proved to be one of the most thrilling visits of all. When we got aboard, the mate was sitting on top of the deckhouse piecing the great outer jib. That sail had been ripped in a gale, and they had taken it off the jibboom to mend it. The mate had a huge rope-needle, and he wore a regular sailmaker's thimble, which is a small metal disk set in a leather strap worn around the wrist. He was putting in a strip of new canvas, which looked very clean and white in contrast to the other. We had a little talk; then I played about the ship as usual, climbing along her bulwarks — in fact, literally skipping and running along her bulwarks, to Mother's terror. Then, after I had climbed up to the crosstrees two or three times, always looking rather longingly at the topsail ratlines, Captain Avery asked us if we would like to eat supper with him, aft, at four bells (six o'clock). Mother called me down from some high perch and asked me. Would I eat a meal on a real ship? Would I indeed!

So down we went, into the room where the massive table was hooked up to the wall. Before that I had become well acquainted with the cook, a delightful old man who told us he was up in the seventies somewhere. (You may believe it or not, but his name was Oscar Follett.) He was, or at least had been, the best sailor aboard; he had served in real square-riggers, and knew a great deal about them. I called him "matey," and we had a grand time together. Once I had asked him if he wouldn't like me to go with him back to Nova Scotia. I told him I would wash dishes for him. He replied: "Yes, you could help me a lot." For the matter of that, I had even asked the captain — in joke, of course — if *he* wouldn't like me to sail back with him, and I had told him too that I was willing to wash dishes to earn my passage. Said he: "You wouldn't have to wash dishes to go with me!" The cook is very amusing. Right off, then, I had a feeling — a doubtful, vague feeling — that all was not quite right between the cook and the skipper. For the cook, seeing company arrive, was in the process of changing the tablecloth, which was rather begrimed. The captain said: "Oh, don't bother about that, steward — that's all right." Then said the cook very violently: " 'Tain't neither! 'S dirty!" And he yanked it off with one good snatch.

Down we sat, the three of us, to a delightful meal of cold fat ham, boiled potatoes mixed up with corned beef and a kind of greasy gravy, very tough ship's bread, canned pears, and very strong black tea. It was coarse grub — there is no denying it — yet, in the excitement of the moment, it seemed to make everything more romantic and adventurous. I tackled the bread with the determination of one possessed; I hardly heard the cook spinning us a yarn. This is something to the effect of the way he talked:

"The only disadvantage of your comin' along of us when we sail is 'at ye're powerful likely to be seasick. 'Most everyone is seasick for a few days. Me, when I first went to sea, I was seasick ten days, and I lay there in me bunk, and ate nuthin' at all — nuthin' 'cepting a little cold water, an' I'd chuck that right up again. Now, the cap'n I was sailin' with, he was always nice to me, 'n' he didn't see me for ten days, so after a while he come forrard and asked me what was the matter. 'What's the matter with you, Si?' says he. 'Well, sir,' says I, 'I'm seasick. I've been here ten days.' 'Have you eaten anything, Si?' says he. 'No, sir,' says I. 'Well, but, Si, you must eat something, or you'll die. You must eat something, Si. Now come, get out of your bunk, and walk around a bit. So I got out of my bunk, and I was so weak that he had to put his arm around me, or I should have fallen over. 'Now, Si, ain't there anything you'd like to eat?' 'No, sir, nothing,' says I. 'But, Si, you must eat something, or you'll die.' 'No, sir, I can't eat anything.' 'Now, Si, you jist take it easy, and think if there ain't something I can get you to eat. No, sir, there ain't nuthing.' 'Now, Si, you jist think a minute, and see if there ain't anything.' 'Well, sir,' says I, 'I believe I'd like a little strong cold tea, without any sweetening in it.' So he got up and went and fetched me my quart mug full of tea, and I drank the last drop of it, and it stayed down, too. 'N' I was niver seasick again after that."

(I managed to hear that three times before seeing the last of the steward, and each time it was longer and more complicated, with more details.) All the time, the little old man was leaning up against a projecting panel of the wall, with his arms crossed, glaring and glowering and staring and scowling at the captain. He would arch up his bald forehead, making the high wrinkles show, and his eyes would look most keen and piercing — his old blue eyes — beneath his high forehead. I never saw such expressions of hatred in my life; and I confess that I was amused very much indeed. And when Captain Avery looked at the steward to ask him for something, he, too, looked frowningly and hatefully. But the cook was fond of me, partly because I listened to his talk with a long ear, and partly because I had helped him, to my own delight, setting the table and getting the supper ready.

WE were through before very long, and the mate and bo's'n came down to take our places at the table. The most exciting part of the evening was still to come; it was indeed. No sooner was I out on deck than I scurried again up into the rigging. I never got so used to climbing the rigging that I could treat it as a commonplace matter. It was always thrilling to me, and I felt myself growing more and more a sailor. By this time the whole crew knew that I liked to climb around and that I was daring about it, and usually I could see one or two, especially the old cook, looking out of the galley or the fo'c'sle, grinning up at me. I was no longer in their world: I was at the level of the sea gulls.

But on this trip up to the crosstrees I had a new idea in my head — those quivery, frail topsail ratlines. They tempted me hugely. I felt that my climbing in the rigging was very imperfect until I could say that I had been on the topmost of those additional rope steps. This time, when I reached the crosstrees, I didn't pause at all. I was afraid my idea might not work. I gripped for those shrouds right off, and I went right up those shaky ropes. They were hard to climb, too, because I didn't quite dare do them from the outside, where, of course, they would have been a great deal easier. Instead, I went up from the inside of the rigging, so that I was climbing at a very awkward angle. But I went on up, until I stood, quivering and shaking, on the topmost rope. I felt as if I were adding more and more steps to my brilliant sailor record. So I was quite proud and delighted when I came down from the ratlines. I went and talked a moment to the cook, who had been sitting on the starboard bulwarks amidships, watching. He immediately said to me: "Why didn't you go right on up to the truck?" "I see no footropes," said I. "Well," said he, "you might have shinned right up." "Oh, I imagine I'll come to that in time," I answered.

But now I had an even more exciting idea in my mind. I went back to the mate and told him I was going out on the bowsprit. "I'm going out as far as I can," I said. "I don't know whether I'll get any farther than the jibboom, but I'll get out to those footropes anyway."

"Well," said he, "just be careful to hold on to that wire rope, and you'll be all right."

So I started. I crawled, step by step, out along that three-inch shelf on the side of the bowsprit, holding fast to the indicated rope. Once the furled jib, which was loosely a-swing amid its tackle, lumbered outwards toward me and nearly pushed me off the bowsprit; but, happily, I ducked under it and went on. As I walked along that shelf, I felt that I could not possibly keep on climbing out so successfully; it was incredible that I should be able to walk so far without any mishap. Yet I reached the frail footropes of the jibboom in safety. Cautiously I stepped down upon them, and they sagged deeply beneath me. From knot to knot I edged, bracing my feet upon the crossropes. Without them I could never have made my way out, because the jibboom was tipped uphill so steeply. And at each step I felt new surprises. Why didn't something happen to stop me? Why didn't I go suddenly hurtling down into the sea so far below? Was I actually going to be allowed to reach the very end? After a little breathless maneuvering, I did reach it — the very white painted tip of the jibboom, which is one of the most romantic inches of wood in the world. Holding on to the forestay, I stood up and smiled a smile of triumph.

The Voyage of the Norman D.

Then I had one of the strangest surprises of my life. It was time for the factory workers to be getting out, and, when I stood up and looked over to the road, there was an audience of at least fifty people, of all ages and sexes, leaning over the bridge and looking at me. Some of them waved and grinned. How like a sailor I felt! Then, cautiously, but not quite so slowly, I edged down the jibboom again, always being careful to brace my feet on the footrope knots so that I shouldn't slip. When I got back I will not deny that I skipped, danced, ran, flew, all the way down the bulwarks until I reached the taffrail, where I leaped down.

Gradually my reputation was increasing. I was climbing rung after rung of the ladder of sailor fame. I was so gay that I skipped about among mate, cook, and captain, asking the names of ropes and things. I learned quite a lot that evening. But I had more delights coming to me: I still had great duties to perform about the deck. The mate was running about, getting everything ready for the night. The main gaff was hoisted, having been used to swing the main cargo up from the hold and over the side of the ship, where the men working in the lumber trucks had unfastened it. So the gaff had to be lowered. That was where the main part of my work came in. I held the peak halyards; the mate, on the other side of the ship, held something else — I could not see what, but in all probability the throat halyards. The mate came over and said to me: "You want to be a sailor man? See, now, hold this rope, and let it out very slowly." So I took the rope, and I let it out slowly, hand over hand. Slowly the gaff came down, and I felt an enormous weight pulling at the rope, so that sometimes it pulled itself more quickly than I wished through my hands, burning them. Once it almost got free from me, and I saw it whizzing along. I heard a cry from the mate, and with a little strength I managed to stop it. There was a small bang and the gaff came to rest.

Then a rope had to be uncoiled from the mainsail boom, which the mate wanted to use to make the gaff fast. We uncoiled it together, one on each side of the boom, and pulling the rope across hand over hand — I pulling, the mate loosening the coils. Several times I got the rope's end in my face with a smart little *smack*! but that was sailorly, and I minded it no more than the dirt.

After that I helped the mate by carrying coils of rope which he wanted moved, and doing other small jobs. By this time Mother was saying that it was time to go home; so after the mate had finished his work I said to him: "Oh, how I wish I could go along back to Nova Scotia!" and left the schooner.

* * *

I DON'T remember whether or not we visited the schooner any more before a certain memorable day, only a few days before she sailed. It was on a Saturday. I had been talking steadily about the schooner to everyone; I had described in full detail my various accomplishments to my old friend Mr. Rasmussen; I had thought more about the beauty and the adventures of the *Norman D.* than I had ever thought about anything before. And this Saturday morning, more than two weeks after the schooner had come in, the fever which was in me for sailing became intolerable. I shall never forget — never, though I live to be a thousand — how I felt that morning. I strode up and down the porch, feeling, ranting, and looking a good deal like a lion just brought in from the jungle, caged. I was frantic — wild — unpersuadable. I said: "You can't keep me from it — you can't, you can't — I'm going to sail with the *Norman D.* And I'm going up to the dictionary *now* to learn the thirty-two points of the compass by heart, so that I shall be well prepared, and so that I shall be allowed to steer. Yes, I'm going with the schooner!"

"But you can't go alone."

"I can! I can! I must! I shall die if I don't. Of course I can. Of course! I know the captain well, and the mate, and the cook, and the bo's'n, too, for that matter. Oh, don't talk to me — I'm going; I must go!"

"But how can you get back?"

"Oh, Lord! I am wild, and I am crazy, but I'm not so wild that I can't think that out. You know the *Norman D.* is going to load up at Bridgewater; then she sails for New York; and Daddy can meet her at New York when she comes in. Oh, don't try to talk to me, or keep me from it, because you can't. You can't do it. No! I'm going to sail."

What a wretched, cruel thing *reality* is — one of those hideous monsters which ill-fated Pandora let out of her magic chest!

"Now, Bar, be reasonable. You know you can't go without someone else to go along too, and look out for you — someone we know."

"But we do know the captain, and the mate, and the cook."

"Yes, but not intimately. Now, listen a minute, and I'll tell you something."

"Not a word, unless you give me permission to go. And if you don't give me permission, I'll go without. I'll run away, I will, and be a stowaway aboard the *Norman D.* And, if that's the case, what's more, I shan't return home at all. I shan't come back to New York. I'll stay aboard her all the time. Indeed I will! And I'll live the life I'm made to live. — Oh, if I were only sure I had a sailor stomach!"

"That's right, too: you'll certainly be seasick."

"What do I care? Do you think you can break me of my desire to sail just by telling me I'll get seasick? To be sure I'll be seasick. And, what's more, I'll get over it, too. Now, may I go, or must I go without leave?"

"Now, listen again. You can go if you get someone to go with you. And if you can't get someone to go with you, you just cannot go with the schooner, that's all. That's definite — you cannot sail with her unless someone goes with you. But you can go out on the tug to see her set sail — "

"Oh! I could never stand to see her sail away without me."

"And you can go with her some other trip — perhaps on her next trip — "

"But she has no schedule, and she only comes into New Haven very rarely."

"No matter. Perhaps you can sail with her from New York the next time she comes in there."

"But by that time I may not want to sail any more."

"Well, that's absolutely the best that can be done. If you can get someone to go with you, you may sail; if not, no."

"And so now I'm going to learn the points of the compass."

"But wait! Not so fast! Supposing you can't get anyone to go?"

"Why, then I'll go alone, and heaven help me!"

"No, you won't go alone."

"Well, I'm going to learn the points of the compass, anyway, because it may take me a long time to learn them all — and I shan't mind knowing them anyway, whether I go or not. But I'm going! I'm sure of it. Something tells me so."

* * *

SO I fled upstairs to the dictionary and looked up the points of the compass. After about fifteen minutes of hard studying, I could stand off from the dictionary and repeat them all, slowly and rather hesitatingly, from north clean round to north again.

In five more minutes I could say them off quite smoothly, and before I got downstairs I could run them off pretty fast — though I still had to think hard about them. Now I can reel them off as fast as the names of the sails of a square-rigger. They are nothing but second nature to me. All the morning ran through my head: "North, north by east, north-northeast, northeast by north, northeast, northeast by east, east-northeast, east by north, east. . . ." (You have no idea how much harder that is to write than it is to say.)

When I appeared downstairs, the family stared at me as though I had gone absolutely cuckoo. In fact, by this time I had not the slightest doubt that I had. I immediately confronted them with "North, north by east," and the rest of it. Then I said: "Now whom do you suggest?"

"For what? To go with you?"

"Ay, ay! What else should I mean? For what else can anyone possibly serve?"

"Bar, are you serious? Is it true that you really want to go so badly as all this, or is it just one of your jokes?"

"Lord! Do I joke? Can't you tell that I am serious? What? Have you never seen me serious before? Or possibly you haven't. Anyhow, don't you know when I'm serious, and when I'm not?"

And through me flowed a stream of the most marvellous sea dreams I have ever known. I thought of having the high white sails puffing with wind over my head. I thought of a great ship leaning over, I thought of pirates, buried treasure, mystic isles. I thought of the delight of sailing, not to New York or Boston, but to Nova Scotia — a strange country, new to me. I thought of the companionship I might develop with the crew. I thought of the storms, gales, perhaps even typhoons, I might encounter. I thought of the stories I should have to tell when I came back, swinging to and fro in my sailor walk, sunburned, brawny, knowing everything about the ropes which looked as numerous to my inexperienced eyes as sea shells on the seashore. I thought of how strange it was that, only two weeks ago, I had considered the whole thing well-nigh an impossible dream, and of how, now, here I was on the point — perhaps — of sailing myself.

* * *

TO BE reasonably brief with the matter, there was a whole lot more talk, but eventually it was decided that, if I could get G. S. Bryan to go as my shipmate on this adventure, the chances were all in favor of my going — that is, if Captain Avery assented. Otherwise the chances were distinctly unfavorable. And so, after a lot of complicated long-distance telephoning, I communicated the idea to the Bryans and got them to come over Sunday (the next day) to talk it over with us and with Captain Avery.

Of course, I spent most of my time skipping wildly around the house, shouting out "North, north by east . . ." and other ship words. Also, I spent a good deal of time with my face buried in the dictionary, learning new words and names, so that I should not be landlubberly when I went off sailing in that schooner. Off sailing — think of it! My dreams realized so soon — so soon!

Well — and this is leaving out a great, great many details — the Bryans did come over on Sunday, and we all went down to assault Captain Avery. The old skipper was most entertaining that day. He spread out all his charts on the dining room table and showed us his various passages, and by which way he would go up to Nova Scotia, and which way he had come on *all* of his previous trips; and, of course, that involved us in listening to a great many tales of all kinds. I really thought the man was powerless to stop talking. He spread out chart after chart, and explained them all to us — all the various things which the mysterious little signs indicate. This was a whistling buoy, that a bell buoy — and so on, absolutely endlessly. (Charts are certainly fascinating. They show the stretches of sea all marked and written up, even more than a land map shows the land. They show soundings everywhere, marks for buoys, lighthouses, and the rest, and also signs which indicate what kind of bottom you are sailing over. As for the land, it is simply blank, just as the sea is in land maps — blank except for a few of the important shore towns.) Then, after they had been rolled up and put away, he fell to telling tales once more. He came into a description of rough weather; and that evidently reminded him to show off his trick furniture, for he immediately put his hand beneath the table and pushed a shutter of some kind, and instantly little racks, crisscrossing each other and running all around the edge, shot up two or three inches above the rest of the table. "It's a very primitive arrangement, folks, but it certainly does come in handy in rough weather."

He pointed to a hook on the wall of the cabin just beside his desk, to which was attached a long string with an empty ink-bottle hanging at the end of it. "Now, folks," said he, "do ye knaow why I hung that up there? Well, I'll tell you. You look very carefully and see 'f you can tell which way the schooner is listing." We all studied the empty ink-bottle for some time in silence. At last Daddy said:

"It strikes me she lists to port a little." "That's right, folks; she lists just a leetle bit to port. Yes, I allus did have an idea that she listed a little."

He described everything in absolute detail. He would tell us exactly what sails he took in or let out during such and such a trip; also exactly how many reefs he took in this sail or that during this or that kind of weather. And some of his pronunciations were delightful. He was continually saying: "Ye knaow, folks . . ." and he always pronounced "route" as "rout."

We fell to giving little hints about our going on the trip back with him. But he was rather obstinate, and persisted in his own material. Some of the hints he would take, and then slyly pass them over, with "Oh, yes, I guess that girl would like to go along with us! I wouldn't mind taking her either, if she had another girl friend to go along with her." This seemed to suggest something like accordance, and we redoubled our efforts. But he persisted gently in his "girl friend" idea, and wouldn't take the most obvious hints. At last we all withdrew from the schooner, except Daddy, who stayed behind, talking. We considered ourselves vanquished in our hopes, and there were some pretty gloomy moments. But Daddy shortly afterwards came tearing out on to the wharf, looking very excited about something or other. "Now you," he said, "you're going to go down to the schooner on Tuesday morning, to find out when she sails. And then you telephone your shipmate here, and tell him when; and then the two of you pile aboard and away to Nova Scotia. And I think I make out that it would relieve Captain Avery of considerable embarrassment if you would take along some blankets."

My head was in a whirl, being mixed up with the captain's indifference to hints and Daddy's explosion of the welcome which the captain had apparently given to the situation when it had been placed before him directly. But the delight that possessed me! I was really going to sail! Yes, in spite of all obstacles, I was going to sail. And not long before that I had thought of sailing only as a vague dream far off in the future; and not long before that I was only beginning to know a few of the simplest things about ships, which were all vague and romantic and fairy-like to me; and not very long before that I didn't know the slightest thing about sails of any kind, and, not knowing, had not cared. But now! Something had suddenly started to open up to me, like a great window overlooking ships and the sea.

And I could not help a few doubts crossing my mind. It was really a bit too good to be true, and I was inclined to disbelieve it a little. For my superstition warned me that something would turn up to keep me from sailing — that an accident might occur aboard, or an accident at home, or an accident that would prevent my shipmate from accompanying me. And, after all, it *was* too good to be true.

YET nothing did occur. The few days flowed on smoothly. On Tuesday morning, as had been previously arranged, Mother and I went down to see Captain Avery and find out when he "calculated on" sailing. We walked down Brewery Street in a drizzling rain, and just before reaching the wharf we encountered the skipper himself, walking up the street to town, with a huge umbrella over his head. We consulted with him, standing there in the rain, for a few minutes. He told us to be aboard the schooner by four bells (six o'clock) that afternoon; he told us to bring blankets, and also any small snacks, such as crackers or fruits, which we might want for luxuries, in case we were seasick. It seemed almost certain that I should go. I didn't see anything standing in the way. Again the romance, the adventure, the piraticalness of it overwhelmed me, and I could not believe my senses. We walked down close to the wharf gate and stood there for a short time, watching them discharge the lath from the bottom of the hold. They were using the main gaff as a crane. They would swing it over the hold, tie several bundles of the lath on to a rope from the end of it, and then swing it out over the lumber carts, where the teamsters would unfasten the bundles. They were working the gaff, of course, by the machinery in the engine-room. I was thinking about the next day, and of being towed out into the open sea; I hardly saw the crew toiling away in the rain, hardly heard the steady drone of the engine.

To my delight, who should be riding back in the same trolley but my old friend Mr. Rasmussen? I fell immediately to telling him all about it. "Well," said I, "the captain says for all hands to be aboard by four bells this afternoon."

"So!" said he. "And you — are you all ready? Have you got your oilskins, sea boots, sou'wester?" "Well, no. You see, I haven't had very much time to get ready. I only decided a few days ago that I would sail with the schooner."

"Why, what kind of a sailor are you?" said he. "You see, mate," I replied, "I haven't yet decided whether I shall enlist as a regular member of the crew. I'm still only a passenger."

We talked some more, about his own sloop, and what the chances were of my having a sail in her sometime. He told us all about her — how he had bought her, and how he had taken her all apart to find out what she was made of and whether she were really seaworthy, and how he repaired her here and there until she was as snug and tight as he could wish, and how now he was not afraid of any weather for her, knowing her to be as strongly made and shipshape as a sailor's heart could desire.

We telephoned, and the Bryans agreed to be over at two bells, so as to have a good margin left over. The day seemed horribly long, I was so wild and excited. After lunch I went to the most tipsy rocking-chair in the house and rocked, and rocked, and rocked — so that I should be ready for a little rolling after meals. I didn't honestly think I should be seasick — but I am a very suggestible sort of person.

There was something darksome and fearful in the air — and, in spite of my common sense, I could not help a vague misgiving. I found myself repeating hotly: "I'm going! Of course I'm going! There is nothing to prevent it."

* * *

IN the early part of the afternoon the telephone rang. I jumped like a madman for it. It was Captain Avery's familiar croaking voice, and I was so startled that my heart sank down into the toes of my boots. He was pleasant, even though he didn't sound as if he were accustomed to telephoning. All he wanted was to know my address and that of my shipmate; evidently he had to register us.

I was indescribably relieved. But the telephone rang again a very few minutes afterward. Again I sprang for it, and again I could feel my heart running downstairs. Again it was Captain Avery. But this time his voice seemed to denote trouble. "Barbara," he said, "do you realize that you will have to have some identification to go into Canada — something to show that you're an American citizen? You're likely to be held up at Boston, coming back, as an immigrant."

"But — but — what sort of identification must I have, Captain Avery?"

"Just a minute." (Pause.) "I think a letter from your father would do, Barbara."

"Hold the line, please, Captain Avery." I was absolutely terrified, now, and I was about to call for help, when another person took up the line and said, in a pleasant, expressionless voice, "Is your father or mother there?"

"Just a minute," I said again — and, at the same time, I heard the voice of Mother answering on the telephone downstairs. For that I was grateful — so grateful! My heart was still going like a perfect sledge hammer, but I had to pick up the upstairs receiver and listen. This is what I heard (or something to this effect, for my brain had gone absolutely crazy, and my senses had forsaken me. I found myself saying: "You fool! Didn't you know all the time that you couldn't — couldn't — couldn't go on this trip? Didn't you know that something would come up? You mean to say you didn't know that it was far too good for yourself?"):

"Do you realize," said the pleasant, expressionless voice, "that an adult male is taking a minor female into a foreign country?"

"Well," said Mother, characteristically, "I hadn't thought of it in just that way, but, now you speak of it, those do seem to be the facts."

But I could listen no more. I couldn't listen — it was like hearkening to my own doom, and I put down the receiver. I afterwards found out that the rest of the talk was simply on the necessity of identification of some kind, and what kind, and the need of going to a lawyer about it, and so on. And here it was, the afternoon I was supposed to sail; undoubtedly the Bryans were now on their way; and it looked pretty black and desperate.

Mother came dashing upstairs and assaulted me: "This is very serious, Bar. It looks as if you mightn't be able to go, after all. We have to go down-town to see a lawyer, and we may not be able to get through in time."

We bustled into good clothes and bustled at full speed down-town, through the same sort of drizzling, melancholy rain that we had had earlier in the day. Even the rain and the dull grayness of the day seemed to predict no good. Yes, everything was going wrong now — everything which, up to half an hour ago, had been going right. What a difference a telephone call may make! It might make, in this case, the difference between a week of the most piratical, adventuresome, glorious days that I had ever known, and a week of gloomy days at home, lamenting the marvellous chance which I had lost through carelessness, and through not having a wider margin of time left over. I was prepared for the blackest. But my piratical fancies did not forsake me altogether, and I dreamed of how delightful it would be if I could leave home suddenly — snooping out, and flying down the street; down to the *Norman D*. Then I should tell my friend the mate all the trouble, and I was sure he would sympathize, and allow me to stay aboard until she sailed back to New York. There he would smuggle me ashore as a bundle of old clothes, and Daddy would pick me up. Everything would go in a mysterious, piratical fashion. It seems strange, but none of us had ever thought of Canada as a foreign country.

AND now I was to be put to the trial of facing one of those formidable persons called lawyers. But the hope of going even now put courage into my heart, and I strode eagerly. We went into Mr. Holbrook's high office feeling very queer indeed. In that place I looked for no surprise; but one exciting thing did happen. When I went desperately over to the window to get a little light, if not air, while Mother was stating, in her most pitiful tones, the entire case, I saw, over tier after tier of roofs and high buildings, the blue water of the bay, and, looking like a child's toy dock, the old, broken wharf, and, lying alongside it, like a child's toy ship, the *Norman D.*, mirrored in the calm water, white, noble, with her beautiful tall masts towering up against the sky. While Mr. Holbrook was in some of his most solemn moments of discussion, I shrieked out: "Oh, look! There's the schooner now! See, down there by that tiny little wharf. That's the *Norman D.* See? Isn't she beautiful?" At the same time Mr. Holbrook was dictating the necessary affidavit to his secretary. It had to be signed by each of us; and it had to be certified and sealed by the Clerk of the Superior Court; and arrangements had to be made for my birth-certificate to be mailed to Nova Scotia for us on the return trip. While Mother took care of these grave matters, I was dashing furiously homeward in the first trolley, to arrive before the Bryans, if possible, and explain the whole complicated mess to them. And again I fell into my dreams of adventure. It happened that the Bryans had not arrived when I got home, but they had called up from Derby, and been told as much as the house knew about it, and that had put them into confusion, and I was very much afraid that they had gathered from the report that they weren't to come at all. What a grand mess that would be! But they did come, soon after Mother, and again the mess was gone through, and pored over, and thought about. We felt truly safe and sound, having such a ponderous affidavit with us; we did indeed! " . . . By and with the full consent of the deponent . . . "!

We drove down to the schooner to find out for sure whether she was to sail that afternoon or the next morning. We hoped it would be in the morning, because we were very much crowded and confused, and rather giddy with so many accidents and telephone calls and lawyers and affidavits, and we wanted time to get settled down a little and to think things over, and to buy crackers and fruit as Captain Avery had suggested. But I, secretly and against my common sense, hoped to sail right then. I was furiously eager to get away from New Haven and all its traps and snares. Also, I feared that, if I had to spend another night at home, I should be so excited that I shouldn't sleep. I should be so full of ideas about the sea, and ships, and pirates, and adventures — and the trip, the actual trip that I was going on — that I *knew* I shouldn't sleep a wink.

We drove down in the same sort of rain we had been having all day. We told everything to Captain Avery; also Mother, following one of Mr. Holbrook's numerous advices, asked him

The Voyage of the Norman D.

if he would please write a note to certify that we really were his passengers, on board his schooner, from New Haven to Bridgewater. This note we should present to the officials at Boston if challenged.

But we found, to everybody else's joy and my dismay, that the schooner was not to sail until Wednesday morning. Tired and confused and a little dizzy, I ran about among the various members of the crew — especially the cook and mate — and told them, with huge glee, that I should be sailing with them. The cook, good old soul, seemed very much delighted, and at once retold his favorite yarn about the cold tea. The mate said he was sure I should make a splendid sailor.

Glorious! But I need not repeat my new dives into even more wonderful sea dreams. Now, for the first time, I could really shake off the misgiving; now I really knew that I was to do what I had, though for so short a time, longed to do. We ate supper downtown. When I got home to bed, instead of lying awake and tossing, and becoming feverish from excitement, I dropped like a stone into a deep, dreamless sleep. I never slept more soundly in my life — except, perhaps, afterwards, when — but wait a page or two.

THE day dawned fair, and there seemed to be a breeze where we were, for white fair-weather clouds were scudding across the sky. I woke rather early; I was wide awake in a flash, and I leaped out of bed, clapping on my old clothes as hastily as I could. My hair I braided up tightly, as I always do when I go on any wild enterprise. Mother fussed a little over the braids, and said I looked like a hobgoblin. I said that braids were nautical, and befitted the schooner and the sea.

We took three jars of our own homemade orange

marmalade, some of which was to go to the men in the fo'c'sle, the rest aft. We thought this would please Captain Avery. Then, with my sailor rags fluttering about me like a proud banner of triumph, Mother and I marched down Armory Street to the trolley. Mother left me down-town to wait for the Bryans and to buy those everlasting crackers and fruits, but I simply *couldn't* wait, and I transferred into another trolley and sailed down Chapel Street. I was so absorbed in my own dreams that I almost went past Brewery Street. But I saw the topmasts of the schooner just in time, and got out. I couldn't resist saying to myself: "Oh, thank heaven! She is still there." You see, my superstition tried its hardest to make me believe that I still might possibly be hindered from going. It was still trying to make me see imaginary obstacles. But I didn't see any, and I wouldn't see any, and I went tearing down Brewery Street, vaulted lightly through the little gate, and reached the side of the ship, with my suitcase and the three jars of marmalade.

But — what is this? Is my superstition right after all? Are there still more difficulties? It seemed so, for not a soul stirred on deck. I stood there, gazing at the ship, with my suitcase in one hand, and my heart again sinking into my boots. I was just about to raise a hail, as I had done once before, when a sailor-like man, in a blue cotton shirt with the sleeves cut off at the shoulders — he was very brown, almost coppery, with terrific muscles — strode up to me and asked if I wanted to go aboard. He hopped aboard, brought a ladder instantly, and lowered it over the side.

In no time I was having delicious conversations with the cook, who was telling me he was sure I should be seasick, while the mate sat on the bulwarks on the other side of me, telling me he thought I shouldn't be. The mate and the cook fell into a sort of playful arguing, and finally they laid a wager on me — the mate wagering a quarter that I shouldn't be seasick, and the cook wagering his quarter that I should.

The delight of it! Already, this intense familiarity with the crew — and two of them wagering about my seasickness! I could contain myself no longer. I slipped down off the bulwarks and ran to the foremast shrouds; then up on to the bulwarks again and up the ratlines, quick as a squirrel, hand over hand. There I sat on the crosstrees, in the blazing morning sun, watching three or four of the crew who were out on the jibboom replacing the repaired outer jib.

When I came down, the mate and the cook were still talking where I had left them. The mate began to compliment me again on my daring aloft. He told me about one of the crew, Richardson, who had never been much good as a sailor, and who couldn't climb nearly so well as I. We watched that same Richardson, a foolish-looking lad, going up the port main rigging on some little task, and he seemed, indeed, very timid and scared. He turned almost white when he was ordered up, and he went very slowly and cautiously. It was perfectly true that he couldn't climb so well as I. Then the mate came back to my seasickness. The cook had gone back into the galley, and evidently the mate wanted very much to argue in favor of his wager, and strengthen his side a little. So he said to me: "Now, 't ain't likely as you'll be seasick. And, if you are, you'll certainly get over it in a couple o' days. As long as you've a good head, that makes all the difference in the world. Now, Richardson here, he hasn't got a head — he can't stand the height, and he gets seasick every trip. But you look at the way you go scrambling up to the crosstrees. Them as can climb like that never get sick."

We talked about the trip, and what time the captain thought he should be getting out. The captain was then ashore, collecting the last provisions, and they were all anxiously awaiting him and the tug which was to tow us out of the harbor. It was, of course, dead calm in there, but there was a line of vivid blue out beyond, and it looked like a breeze. I asked the mate, in order to air my knowledge a bit, if four bells had yet struck. But the mate evidently saw my trap and thought that I was talking about what I knew nothing of, and he queried in a tone of obvious scorn: "What is four bells?" And I was proud to reply without the slightest hesitation: "Ten o'clock, mate."

* * *

BUT now, in spite of the pleasure of sitting and yarning with my matey, I began to think over again the delight, the impossibly delightful idea, of the voyage. And I fairly squirmed and itched all over. Of course I was impatient for the return of the captain. Shortly he appeared, with a large and mysterious-looking bundle under his arm. Said he to Mother, who was standing on the wharf: "I bet you cant guess what I've got here!" and he chuckled mysteriously.

"No; what is it?"

He chuckled some more. "Well, I'll tell you! I've got two brand-new *pails*, in case they get seasick!"

To myself I was thinking: "Supposing we fool you? Then your new pails would go to waste, wouldn't they?" For I was secretly pretty sure I should be steady. I talked a little to the captain, asking him what time he thought we should be under way, and how soon he expected the tug; for now everything was ready, and we were to slide out to sea as soon as the tug appeared. The mate got up instantly when the captain drew near — not to be caught idling, I suppose — and began to busy himself about the deck. That man has a marvellous knack of finding things to do. When he feels like working, he can always find a thousand little jobs to do here and there.

The Voyage of the Norman D.

Mother came aboard, too, and talked with the captain and the mate. The mate was extraordinarily pleasant, telling her all about what a fine climber I was and what a good head I had, and saying that he didn't think I would be sick. A man had come from town along on to the wharf — seemingly a very nice person, dressed in city clothes. He leaned over the bulwarks, talking to Mother, and telling her how he loved to see the schooners that still came into New Haven now and then, and how rare they were now, and how lucky I was to be sailing with the *Norman D.*, and how soon he'd go if he had the chance.

And, amid all these happenings, the tug which was to tow us out to sea had chugged up slowly, and now lay alongside the schooner to port. There was shouting and *yoho*-ing among the two crews, and through the confusion could be heard the hoarse, loud voice of Captain Avery, rapidly giving his orders. He seemed to me to have a clear idea of what he wanted done, but, if a moment were lost in the execution of his orders, he immediately became nervous and hectic. Towropes were got out and thrust through the cable-holes. Now our mate had skipped ashore and loosened the ropes which held the ship to the posts on the wharf; then he called out to me to untangle the rope where it was snarled around the capstan. Shortly afterwards I was sent to coil it up in a snug, neat coil.

Now everything was astir. The schooner was securely made fast to the tug by a long, stout towrope. This was let out, and the schooner began slowly, slowly to move from the wharf. Now she was quietly turning upon her heel, and soon she was headed out for the open sound, past the breakwaters, past the lighthouses. I felt her sliding on beneath me. There were several little yachts and small sailboats in the bay: they turned and stared at us as we went gliding past. Beautiful indeed we must have looked — but of that I was hardly thinking; indeed, I was thinking of few things, my head was in such a whirl with the delight of the moment.

The wharf grew more and more distant, and the smoking town, too. I was glad to realize that, at length, we were leaving it behind and were bound for the open, free sea and the wild winds and waves. Now we saw East Rock and West Rock as small nubbins of hills in the distance. The tug was to stay with us until we had rounded the tip of a long green peninsula which jutted out into the bay. Beyond this I could still see the bright blue which seemed to denote wind. Now the tug had reached full momentum, and the great schooner was gliding pretty swiftly through the water. More and more distant grew the land behind us — nearer and nearer the open sea.

I was called back to myself by the sudden sound of an engine running. The bo's'n had started our engine, and now the sails were to be run up. Oh, was it true? Could it possibly be true that we were going to run up sails? that there really were a few sails left in this modern world? I heard the voice of Captain Avery giving orders. "Mainsail up first — then foresail, forestaysail, and jibs — put up the spanker and topsails last. Lively there, boys!" And — it was so glorious that I had to pinch myself and rub my eyes hard — the peak halyards were wound around the winch on one side of the engine-room, and the throat halyards around the other, and now, amid the roaring of the engine and the quivering of the great tackles, up went the gaff slowly, quivering and shaking; up went the sail, spreading out gracefully, as white hoop after white hoop ran up the tall mainmast. Up and up and up! Then the mainsail was stretched to its full length, and the gaff came to rest just below the crosstrees. Never had I realized what a vast expanse the sails have. The halyards were made fast. And now the foresail, too, shivering and groaning, began to reach up. It, too, was soon made fast. And then the beautiful jibs, two at a time, went rolling up, their long points seeming to reach into the sky itself. The first two were the forestaysail and jib, the last the flying jib and outer jib. The schooner shuddered. The engine had awakened her; the sea had called, and she was answering.

We were now almost out of the bay. A gentle puff of wind rose, and I saw the great white sails lifting and filling. Then, when the wind died down, they collapsed. And now we had cast the towrope. The tug fell away. We felt like a queen on the ocean, dominating the little boat proudly. Now the tug circled, wheeled about, and started for the wharf again. The *Norman D.* ran up her spanker, the largest sail of all, headed her nose for the open, and began to sail gently on with a steady little breeze puffing out the sails. We were off! We were headed for who knows what strange and mysterious adventures?

ABOUT the first thing we did was to have dinner. We went below aft, and fed on the same sort of sailor grub that Mother and I had had the night we ate supper there. I was sorry that I had to break up the delight by having dinner, and I finished hastily, and went back on deck as soon as possible. Yes, we were sailing. The bo's'n was at the wheel. I talked to him a while. The wind seemed to be rising just a little bit. I tried my best to make the schooner seem to be rolling, but all I could see was a slight waving of the horizon up and down; I couldn't feel it at all. But the sails were full and steady, and oh! so beautiful they seemed to me. I could see myself entering into the spirit of sailing right off. I had the most curious sensations I have ever experienced — of mystery, of adventure; I can't describe it at all. But I could think myself a sailor. The crew were now unfurling the topsails. When they were all loosened, the topsail halyards were hauled, and up went the topsails, one at each topmast, sharp mountain-peaks on the lower sails.

But, thought I, I mustn't neglect my duty through sheer delight. I ran up to the galley, had a talk with the cook about almost everything under the sun, and dried his dishes and helped clean up the galley for him. He thanked me cordially and very touchingly, and I resolved to help him a great deal. He seemed like such a sad little old man! I never knew quite what to make of him. The arched wrinkles upon his high, bald forehead, his smallness and robustness, all combined to make him a very curious-looking specimen. He wore, too, a sort of butcher's apron arrangement, and somehow the strings dangling behind always seemed comical to me. But he knew more about ships than anyone there, and he seemed rather disgusted at the greenness of this young crew. "Oh, Lordy, Lordy," he would say, "that crew — they give me a pain. Why, in old days, when the sails were much harder to hoist up, and when all the work was a cursed sight harder — why, we poor sailors would get flogged and fired fer bein' so slow as on this schooner. And here, they have an engine and everything made to suit them, yit they dawdle and lazy around and don't seem to know how to do nothing."

There seemed now to be quite a breeze outside. I could somehow feel the deck sliding from beneath me, and I staggered around in the galley, much to the amusement of the cook, who put his hands on his hips, and roared aloud, and told me I hadn't got my "sea legs on yit." I stepped out of the galley to see what the weather was doing. It was sparklingly clear. The sun made mazes of color on the blue sea. The wind *was* coming up, and I could see the waves sloshing against the side of the schooner. We were slipping down along the coast of Rhode Island, a low green bar far off. The ship was leaning gently and quietly before the rising wind.

The sails looked fuller and puffier than ever, and the breeze was very fresh and delightful. I returned to the galley and said: "Well, there seems to be quite a breeze out, cook." But the cook was not to be fooled with a landsman's idea of a breeze. And he replied in a truly pathetic tone of voice: "Oh! Oh! There's such a terrible wind out — I'm seasick!" and he laughed and laughed.

The dishes were finished very shortly. I went on deck and sat and watched the sea. I had such a marvellous sense of remoteness! In spite of the long green coast, I could not help feeling that we were out in mid-ocean — and when I turned my back to that edge of land I was sure of it. The sea seemed to stretch away boundlessly. The sky was of a marvellous color, but away off on the horizon there were banks of clouds, casting weird and lovely shadows down on the far skyline — maroons, wine-colors, green, and dark, dark blue. Very strange! And the sails seemed white — oh! so white — in spite of the fact that they were somewhat dirty with rough handling.

The wind was steadily rising all the time, and the schooner keeled over gently and quietly, more and more, on her starboard side. When I ran to the starboard bulwarks to look down into the waves, all I saw was the raging white bone which the schooner carried proudly in her white teeth — a mass of foam, white, whiter than fresh-blown snow, curling into gorgeously weird and beautiful shapes, with a rushing noise as its small bubbles went out, thousands at a time. How angry the sea was becoming! The waves rose high and high — ten times higher than in any gale I had ever fought in the canoe. The waves roared, the wind moaned, the whitecaps rose up mysteriously like snow-palaces and then subsided again. All this time the sea was becoming overcast with clouds, and now the waves were shadowed and strange. And to see them, in their dark green and blue, with those castles of foam surmounting each wave like proud ivory — oh, this was sailing! And yet it was nothing to what was to come.

The schooner was keeled away over now, but she didn't roll a bit. She was absolutely steady, and kept on her course without varying a quarter point, straight as an arrow. I shall never forget the delight with which I went to the fo'c'sle deck, where I sat as far as I could squeeze into the peak of the bow and looked down on the port side, where the raging sea seemed far, far below; and then down on the starboard side, where it was near, and angry, and lapping furiously at the ship, and reaching hungrily for it. And from there I could look down straight ahead and see the foam, I could see where the sharp cutwater divided the seas in half, and I could see one long chain of foam reaching down the port side and another down the starboard — each of them like a range of towering snow-capped mountains. And three or four white-winged gulls swooped and darted about, looking, as they flew low over the waves, like whitecaps themselves.

FOR a good part of the afternoon this kept up. But, alas, towards night I could feel the breeze going down, and the schooner slowly and gradually righted herself, and the sails were close-hauled a little to catch every bit of breeze that was coming to us. And then I began to feel the roll. I could see the horizon ahead of us waving up and down. It was a delightful sensation, like that of a seesaw, for the schooner was not pitching, but only rolling head-on. All the same, I was sorry to find the sails flapping. First they would puff out suddenly at a little spurt of wind, then slowly empty again and hang idly flapping. Calmer and calmer it grew, and then the tackle began to rattle and groan: and what a racket it did make!

The Voyage of the Norman D.

I believe there is no other din aboard a sailing vessel that is anywhere nearly so loud, tiresome, or monotonous as that which the tackle makes in a calm. First the sails would swing out to the full stretch of their sheets, either when the schooner rolled forward or when a tiny spurt of wind suddenly rose; then they would bring up short against the sheet with a terrific groaning as the ropes became taut with a jerk; then, on the return, the booms would swing back in again and every bit of breeze would go out of the sails. They would flap, and billow and roll uncannily, with the reef points jigging about like live creatures. This would go on while the schooner rolled back, and then, as she dived forward again, the sails jerked back on the full reach of the sheet. The sails would fill for a brief moment, and during that moment each reef point would tap its tip upon the taut canvas, each at a slightly different time, so that there was a sort of *purr-r-r-r-r-r-r*! and almost at the same time the sails would relax. Again they would billow and flap, and again swing back inwards. And a terrible creaking and groaning was going on all the time, until, if you listened to it, it would almost drive you crazy.

The schooner was now rolling deeply. Below in the cabin, everything was banging about. The inside of it was so much more like a house than the deck was, that I could scarcely persuade myself I was on a ship; and it seemed strange to feel a house rolling and swinging.

The air, in spite of the calm, remained clear and sharp, and there was a glorious sunset. Long fingers of fire reached out in fan-like shapes from the horizon, and the sky was all flushed with rose. To see a sunset from a schooner! We were so enchanted with our new kind of life that we stayed up very late that night. It grew dark quickly; night came down upon us like a sudden black cloud, and it grew cold. A breeze came up — just enough to hold the beautiful great sails steady as though they had been carved of marble, and to make a glimmering pair of foam-wings along the sides of the ship.

It was then, standing by the wheel in the dark, that I had my first real talk with the mate. It was also the first time I thought of him as piratical-looking. He was, when I stopped to think about it, the most piratical-looking person I ever laid eyes upon. He is very dark and swarthy, with luxuriant black hair and eyes the most wicked-looking on earth; wicked, yet strangely playful at the same time, and with a curious twinkle which shows when anything amuses him. And he is a silent, mysterious, soft-footed person, who looks as though he were brooding dark and treacherous things — perhaps concocting a mutiny. And, standing there in the dark, his pirate face sharply silhouetted against the brightness of the starry sky, he made me feel as though I were cabin-boy on a pirate ship. But this is looking at him from only one side. In the morning, and on sunny days, one wouldn't suspect that he was piratical. There is only a hidden suggestion of it — a faint smile of treachery in his eyes, and something that is evil in his chuckle. It is on foggy days, and in the late of the afternoon when it begins to grow dark, that the pirate in him shows. He is the one for us to sail with, Alan, if we ever start off on a treasure-expedition!

WHEN I saw the stars, I had a strange experience. In spite of the small breeze which kept the sails from making their infernal racket, there was quite a roll and swing and swoop to the ship; she dipped her prow like the wings of a sea gull. But when, looking up at the high stars, I picked out one bright one above the truck of the mizzen-mast, and was just beginning to try to identify it, I saw it swinging about the mast in bewildering and beautiful curves and flashes of gold; and, to my puzzled eyes, it seemed to leave a burning track behind it. I have seen shooting stars; I saw one two years ago which glided very slowly and softly across the northern half of the sky — so slowly that I could watch every motion of it. And my first thought was that this revolving star was a specially magical shooting star. But I never saw a shooting star make bewildering curves and circles. I looked at the other stars, and they all seemed to be gyrating crazily about the sky, sometimes fast, sometimes slowly. And then I could feel the mighty ocean throbbing beneath me, and again I looked at the mast, and it seemed stock-still against the wheeling sky; yet I could feel the schooner rolling and pitching in the swell. Of course, the sky was just as it ought to be: it was the mast, the schooner, that rolled as the sea heaved.

The moon had not yet risen, and everything was pitch dark except for magical sparks of starlight. All the afternoon we had been continually passing small steamers and barges, and I had never thought they were beautiful until now. I was too devoted to my original idea of vessels with sails to pay much attention to little "chuggers," as the crew often called them. But now, at night, they suddenly became fairy-like. A small steamer would click slowly by across our bow, with a swash of foam, and she looked like an enchanted ship out of some mysterious land of stars. Then a long string of barges passed us far ahead, all towed by a small power boat, and each one gleaming with red and green and yellow lights. One after another they passed, at even intervals, until we had begun to think that there would never be an end to them. And when they had gone, we were again alone in the darkness, except for the far-away lights on shore.

I ran up forward as soon as it was dark, to watch Roy set our side lights. These are large, strong lanterns, one red, one green, which are set in cases a few steps up the rigging. The green one is to starboard, the red to port. They cast mysterious color-shadows on to the sea by our sides.

Then the captain began to tell us about the small power boats known as "rum-chasers." You are likely to see them at any time, cruising about and keeping an eye on all the sea traffic. Sometimes, he said, they board a schooner and examine her cabins and cargo. We had seen several of these boats ploughing at terrific speed through the waves, piling up mountains of foam. One of them now speeded up to us through the darkness and cast a powerful searchlight upon our stern, apparently to read our name. And those long rays shone out strangely in the darkness. Then the boat wheeled about and tore off, diving and rearing and plunging.

And now I began to see a strange, soft light over in the east. I watched and watched, and then I began to see the top of the full moon's circle. Up and up she came, huge in the darkness, and shining like sunlight on snow. I had often dreamed of sailing by moonlight. And now my dreams were realized. Now the breeze held everything quiet, and, except for the swing and roll of the ship and the rushing of the foam divided by her cutwater, everything was silent — oh, so silent and beautiful!

We were on a long run with the wind on our port beam, so that the sails were blown mysteriously over to starboard. They were so still, so soft and still and rounded, that I could scarcely believe they were full of wind. Of course the binnacle lamp was now lighted; and strange it seemed to be steering by that faint glimmer. And now the moon was rising higher — higher. I looked forward at the front part of the ship, and saw the moonlight full on those taut sails, making the moon's side of them shine like newfallen snow, while the inside was dark, gray, and shadowed. How lovely it was to see them gleaming with that strange light, while on and on they bore us without a sound!

I ran up forward on the fo'c'sle deck. The lookout was sitting there, whistling faintly. It gave me a curious feeling to find him there. Ships had lately become so mysterious that I had actually begun to think such things as two-hour tricks, lookouts, and the like were slightly too romantic to be true — though, in the nature of the case, they *must* be true. And, though I knew that there must be a lookout at night, yet, when I found the man sitting there, alone, on the fo'c'sle deck, I was surprised. This was growing more like the old sailing days with every minute!

I had gone up forward for the simple purpose of looking at those moonlit sails from all parts of the ship. Now I saw the jibs once more from close up; and beautiful they were, rounded with wind, running up their slender points into the sky, and flooded with the snowy moonlight like all the other great, majestic sails. Sometimes their rounded outer sides were huge, dome-like mountains with crowns of snow — mountains whose flanks were shadowed, but whose summits loomed out into the full moonlight. Then I looked over the bow, and saw the foam down there, looking more than ever like two white wings. With the moonlight shining on it, it was ghostly white and curling — moonlight on newfallen mountain snow! The sea itself, very dark green, mysteriously heaving and throbbing, was shadowy except on the eastern side, where the moonlight changed it to a delicate mass of quivering, shifting silver.

WHEN I returned aft, after I had sat there on the fo'c'sle deck in the moonlight for a long time, the mate was standing just where I had left him. Evidently it was his watch on deck. He began talking to me immediately — telling me about what a miserable business sailor life was. "It's all right in summer," he said; "yes, it's real fun in summer when there's no rough weather, but, I tell you, it's a rotten, beastly business in winter. Imagine how it would be to get down the sails in a blizzard, when there's snow and hail and sleet flyin' around so thick you can't see, and when your hands freeze up, and you can't keep warm no matter how many clothes you have on — and when you *have* to stand your four hours, whether you want to or not, no matter in what kind of weather, and when you *have* to be ready for a call, whether it's your watch or not. I tell you, it's no fun. You know, Barbara, I could get plenty of good jobs ashore, with just as good pay as I get here. But — there's somethin' about it, in spite of the hard work, and so on; and I just stay and stay, and I don't seem to leave the sea. So I guess I'm a sailor for life, now!"

I had discovered that Bill was his name, and for fun I always used to call him Mate Bill, because of Billy Bones in *Treasure Island*. I told Bill my opinion of sailing, and how I had always wanted to sail, and how glad I was to see that there still were sailing vessels in the world besides fishing schooners. Also we discussed the weather for tomorrow. I told Bill that I wished we could have a real gale of wind, because I had never been at sea, and had never seen anything in the way of rough weather except some of the breezes we used to have on inland lakes. I told him there would be whitecaps, and good white foam, and black squalls, but that they were nothing compared with even the little wind I had seen that afternoon.

Soon Bill strode over to the port bulwarks and looked down into the water. I looked down, too, and to my surprise there were mysterious sparkles in the sea, close to the side of the ship. They were much like firefly sparkles, except that they stayed longer and faded slowly. Bill didn't know what caused them, but he said that they were always a sign of a strong northeast wind. I expressed my delight and said that I hoped for a terrific gale. Bill thought he would tease a little; he said: "Oh, you want to get there too fast! I guess you're eager to be leavin' us."

"No, it isn't that, mate. I should just like to see some rough weather, never having seen any on the sea."

"And right you are. I should like you to see some weather out here, except that I know you'd be seasick — and then I should lose my quarter!" he added, chuckling slyly. That man has an irresistible chuckle — very piratical and treacherous indeed. "But," he went on, "I don't believe we'll have any really rough weather out here — 'cause it's June, and it's summer, and you almost never get much wind then. But I guess it wouldn't take much to have you call it a gale!"

"No, I guess not."

"You know," he said, "I don't like the idea one bit of a northeaster, 'cause that is exactly the way we're trying to sail — northeast — and it will slow us up a lot."

"Well, that won't be so bad," said I. "Because then I'll have my rough weather, and yet I shan't have to leave you so soon! And I should like very much to see how a big sailing vessel tacks, too."

"Well," said Bill, "you'll see some tacking, all right, if we have a northeast gale."

He talked about the whales which he had seen. He said we were always likely to see one, and that they had seen one seventy-five feet long on the trip down from Nova Scotia. (But I didn't ask whether he had measured it with a tape measure.) He said that there were also a great number of blackfish in the sea, which swam and blew just like whales, but were ever so much smaller.

At last he went back to the life at sea. "I've sailed as cook quite a lot, Barbara, too."

"Which do you like better, being mate or cook?" I asked.

"Well, 't's hard to tell. There's good things to say for both. I kinda think I like bein' mate. The cook's job is a mighty pleasant one, though. He don't have to stand no watch, or git wet 'n' cold in bad weather — he jist sits tight in a warm galley and cooks the meals. You may want t' be mate, but there are some times, I tell you, when you'd like bein' cook. 'T's no fun taking in the sails in winter, in a blizzard; 'n' 't's no fun standin' four hours' watch in freezin' weather."

It was getting on to ten o'clock — four bells — and we turned in, leaving the mate alone with his watch. I think I have never — even on mountain-tops — slept more soundly. The roll was like that of a cradle, and it wasn't enough to be uncomfortable, as it grew to be later — only a gentle, easy motion that put me off to sleep in a flash.

* * *

I WOKE up bright and early, and went on deck. The day started off with just enough breeze to feel fresh and cool and to keep the sails steady. We were passing Martha's Vineyard, and the big island looked very green over on the horizon — a long, rather high green bar, in sudden contrast to the bright sea-blue.

We were now getting into the shoals which Captain Avery had showed us two or three times on the charts. There were buoys, lightships, and lobster-trap buoys everywhere. Every now and then we would pass a lightship with, painted on it, the name of the shoal at which it was stationed. There were odd names — Handkerchief, Half Moon, Stone Horse.

Going down to breakfast with a very good appetite, I couldn't help counting off on my fingers the number of meals I had had without the slightest seasick feeling. The crew were very teasing and bothersome all day about it. They kept asking me, every time I was silent and stood gazing down into the water, whether I were seasick. I laughed — I couldn't become angered with those people whom I had always wanted for companions — took their teasing as a matter of course, and determined to make them respect me later on. I had already won the esteem of the cook. I dried dishes for him again after breakfast. Then I saw that the mate had a broom out and was sweeping the deck. Wishing to be of service, I said: "Don't you want me to help?"

"Do you like to sweep?" said he.

"Sure!" I replied.

He gave a curious, pleased grin and left the broom where he had been working. I picked it up and began, rather deftly, I thought, to sweep in narrow corners of the deck and under coils of rope. I started working down from the port bow; the mate went to fetch another broom and swept down from the starboard bow; and together we made quite brisk work of it. Then the mate fetched a shovel, dumped the debris overboard, and thanked me. Yes, I would show that crew that I was no more afraid of work than any of them.

I rather liked Bob, the bo's'n. The youngest aboard, except possibly Richardson, he had been at sea only two years, but already he had risen in rank. He was a most amusing lad. He told me all about his family, and about himself, and about Bill; and, when I asked him if he didn't like having Bill for a mate (I believe I forgot to say that Bill and Bob are brothers), he replied that it didn't make the slightest difference to him, except that perhaps he didn't get so much blame for things. He is remarkably careless when he is steering. If the captain orders the spanker to be close-hauled, Bob leaves the wheel in mid-air, as it were, and fixes the sail.

He told me that all the other boys made a mess of steering — that they were always turning the wheel this way or that way; but that he found the right position and then let it take care of itself, as it would for some time.

* * *

THE day turned out remarkably exciting. To begin with, my shipmate and I went forward, in the middle of the morning, to talk with the cook, who was sitting sedately in the galley doorway, looking very curious and sad. He seemed mighty glad to have someone to talk to. He rattled on for a while in a delightful way, about this and that and the other thing; really he was much more entertaining than Captain Avery, and he stuck to one subject longer. But I was watching the sea and the sky and the sails, and I didn't pay much attention to him until I heard something that made me prick up my ears.

"As for Captain Avery," he was saying, "I never knew an uglier, more nasty, more contemptible man. I never knew a man that could do one half the mean things he does. Why, he's famed all along the coast of Nova Scotia for being a rascal! I tell you, he's never paid a bill in his life without making a row over it. Why, even the men who came to buy the lumber we brought down — he tried to cheat them out of the few dollars they earned. Now, here, I get sixty dollars a month for cookin' for this schooner. I can't even get that much without some kind of a bally row. And every man of this crew is dissatisfied. If you don't believe me, go ask some of them. They'll tell you what they think of him! You know, I've been cook of this vessel before, and, when the owner enlisted me agin, I didn't want to go. Says I: 'Now I just can't get along with Captain Avery, and I refuse to sail on this vessel while he's skipper.' But the owner says: 'Now, Si, you're all wrong about the captain.' 'He hates me,' says I. 'Now, Si,' says he, 'he told me with his own lips that he thought you was a fine cook, and that he thought very highly of you.' 'Oh, nonsense,' says I, 'I've sailed with Captain Avery before, and I know what I know — he hates me!' Well, the owner coaxed and coaxed, and finally I said I would go, for sixty dollars a month. But Captain Avery don't play fair with me. He tells me to my face he dislikes my cooking. How can I help that, when he won't give a fellow anything to cook with? You wouldn't believe it when I tell you, but I haven't got a drop of flavoring extract of any kind on board this vessel. And he always buys provisions of the very poorest kind — the poorest, cheapest, dirtiest brands of coffee and tea they make. Why, I asked him if he didn't think he ought to get some fancy biscuits or cookies of some kind, for you folks — and do you know what he got? By the Lord, do you know what he got? Uneeda Biscuits! Do you want me to tell you why he never plays the graphophone? 'cause he almost never does. Do you want me to tell you? He's too stingy to use the needles! Once that man was made captain of a Chinese vessel, with a Chinese crew and cook. Before he had been on the ship ten minutes the cook chased him ashore with a drawn cutlass. Do you know why? 'Cause he come nosing around and poking his blasted head into the cook's galley. Now, the galley belongs to the cook, and no one else is supposed to interfere with the cook's work, and it made the Chinese cook mad to see him come interfering. So he just drew his cutlass and chased the man ashore." (I had an idea that it would be untactful to inquire how Captain Avery happened to be in China.)

"Why, I'm very surprised to hear all this about Captain Avery," said I. "When he came up to lunch we thought he was very entertaining and delightful. He strikes me as a very nice old sailor."

It must have taken the cook fifteen or twenty minutes to get the captain denounced to his satisfaction. His voice had been growing louder and more vehement, with more and more small oaths intermingled, and when I interrupted him he was talking with a force that almost shook the galley, so that I felt that it was going to rise up and blow away any minute. I think he would have gone on until supper if I hadn't interrupted.

He soon began again. "So you thought he was a nice old

fellow, did you? Well, I'm surprised. Couldn't you see by the look in the face of him what he was like?"

"Why, no. It struck me he was a very good-looking old fellow — very kind and quiet."

"Well, if you had lived as long as I have, you would know," he went on savagely. "And, I tell you, I seen a fellow that the owner wanted to enlist for a voyage some time back, with Captain Avery for skipper, and the fellow had it all arranged; but when he seen the look in the face of that man, he backed out right off, and said: 'Not me, thanks! Why, to look at that man, I wouldn't sail along of him for a hundred dollars!' and he didn't, neither."

So here was the key to that hatred in the face of the cook whenever he looked at the captain! And immediately we began to see Captain Avery in a new light. We didn't really believe all that had been said about him, but we began to open our ears and eyes and look about us more sharply. We began to hear things which the crew said about him; and we noticed a small, shrill cry, like the peep of a bird, which the bo's'n uttered now and then. At first we had supposed this to be the bo's'n's giggle, but we soon discovered that he was mocking the captain. And, listening closely, we could make out the words of this mockery. Whenever the captain gave an order, the mate, usually in the forward part of the vessel, would repeat it, and then would come this shrill, small, mocking voice of the bo's'n, croaking out the order — echoing word for word everything the skipper had said.

Captain Avery would stand on deck, with his head thrust forward, his back hunched up, and his mouth open. And his voice seemed uglier and harsher than ever to us. Also, he was slightly deaf, and he had an annoying habit of saying "Hey?" every time anyone spoke to him, whether he had really heard or not. This used to amuse us, because when he said that word

"Hey?" he would drawl it out into space, squeezing the last drop out of it; but now it began to annoy us a great deal. We formed a habit of waiting when he said "Hey?" until sure whether he had really heard us or not. Often after "Hey?" he would answer what had been asked him.

* * *

SAD to relate, the wind died down soon before dinner. The sails went through the same noisy tactics as during the afternoon of the first day. I couldn't believe that anything could be noisier than the way they had banged about at that time, but it was nothing to this. We could hardly hear ourselves think, and the inside of the cabin was pandemonium. The doors were banging, dishes were jingling, the whole cabin was swinging back and forth crazily. Through it all the cook was standing very firmly on his two legs, getting dinner ready. If I wanted to stand up for a moment, I had to brace my feet far apart; but the cook was standing at ease, his body yielding gracefully to every motion, while pots and pans were swinging about on the walls, and the tea slopping every which way. As the cook said, I hadn't got my "sea legs on yit." I didn't feel one speck seasick, though the crew redoubled their efforts to irritate me by teasing; and I went dancing down to dinner. But — something about the hotness and stuffiness down below, and the unsteady way in which the chairs were tipping about, and the way the table rose and fell, and the smell — the greasy, fat gravy smell which always saturated the cook's cooking — turned me almost inside out; and, though I ate dinner, I found, just as I was almost through, that I must get out into the open air — there was not a moment to lose! I grabbed the piece of bread and butter which I had been eating, and raced up the stairs without one word of apology or explanation.

The fresh air braced me right up. I didn't get over my weak and dizzy feeling for two or three days, and I ate nothing but oranges and crackers, and those out on deck; but I was never actually sick. I hardened myself during those two or three days; and when the real weather came I minded it no more than dirt. What I did when I began to feel qualmy was to lie down cautiously on top of the deckhouse, in the cool shadow of the sails, and sleep it off. Then I would feel myself for two or three hours; then do the same thing again. In this way I found some very delightful places for naps. My favorite was on the spanker boom — right on the broad saddle of the boom, of course on the windward side of the sail. But this was impossible except in weather when there was enough breeze to hold the sail steady. In calm weather I was often jerked and flapped right off by the sudden reverse motion of the sail, or by the endless tugging and pulling of the boom, or by the way it lifted whenever the sail filled, and then let down with a jerk when the sail emptied. It was fun enough for a short time; but it quickly grew tiring, and I would find a more comfortable place to sleep.

My dizziness gradually wore off, even during the course of that day, and, especially when I did something about the decks, I forgot all about it. The only trouble was that I couldn't go into the galley to dry the dishes for my friend the old cook. As soon as I sniffed the smell of greasy gravy —So I sat in the doorway, poking my head in now and then to talk, and then breathing out into the fresh air again. I have forgotten to say that early that morning the captain had complimented us on our endurance, saying that he had thought we should both be turning our toes up by morning, because of the rolling we had had on the first afternoon.

* * *

The Voyage of the Norman D.

JUST after dinner, as I emerged from the cabin in that mad dash of mine, we saw far off on the horizon a beautiful four-masted schooner coming down from the northeast. What small wind there was was behind us, and it was a head wind for her. She was on the starboard tack. Now, I hadn't realized that at sea there is a definite system of traffic laws among ships. Being on the starboard tack, she had right of way of us, and she crossed our bows very near us, but not so near that we had to heave to. She managed it very neatly, shaving right across clean as an arrow. I was surprised at the progress we were making, in spite of what seemed like the total absence of wind; we approached each other quite fast, and had passed before long. It struck me that the breeze might be coming up a little. Yes, evidently it was, for the sails weren't making so much racket, and the surface of the murmuring ocean seemed bluer and more restless.

The lofty four-master passed us, and we could see that her sails were rippling and banging about like our own. I watched and watched her until she disappeared. If we looked as lovely as she did to us, we must have been a beautiful sight. I noticed that both her helmsman and ours turned their heads and looked at each other.

Bill and I got to talking again about the weather. It struck me that this was a pretty poor apology for the northeast gale which he had promised, and I told him so. He only chuckled, shrugged his shoulders meaningly, and said: "You wait! We'll have a little breeze-o'-wind yet." That phrase, "breeze-o'-wind," somehow always delighted me. Then he added, as a tiny bluish squall, a kitten's-paw, swept over the quiet silver sea: "See! There comes that breeze-o'-wind now!"

The breeze, what there was, swung around gradually into the northeast; but it was light and variable, and it was really hard to tell where it was coming from. We beat and floundered about all the afternoon, making attempts at tacking, though we hardly moved. We kept seeing the same shore line, only it changed its location in a very puzzling way. Sometimes it would be on our larboard bow, sometimes on our starboard, while the ship appeared to be standing still. Sometime during the afternoon a two-topmaster hove in sight and beat about for an interminable length of time, doing as puzzling things as the land — appearing here, and then rising up mysteriously in the other hemisphere, showing now her beam and now her slender bow.

We gave up in despair and dropped anchor. At this I was rather nervous, for the mate had told me how many a sailor who had never been seasick before in his life was likely to succumb when anchor was dropped in a swell. Afterwards the mate told me that he was very sorry for me when he heard that we were going to drop anchor. We rolled about like a bottle. But it didn't bother me. Already I was remarkably on the improve.

Then it struck the captain that the wind seemed to be coming up and swinging around to its former position. After a few hours of lying there we started the engine and hauled up the mudhook. I was interested to see how this was done, and I went forward to watch. The mate leaned far over the side, watching the cable like a cat — giving orders, and stopping the winch every time the chain managed to get fouled, or when anything else went wrong. The head of the anchor slowly appeared through the sea, as that huge rusty chain inched up slowly, disappearing into the cable-hole. Then the head of the anchor lifted its uncanny, sea-ghostlike arms out of the water, dripping, and looking like the risen skeleton of a drowned pirate. Then the whole great mudhook rose up, accompanied by the roaring of the engine, until the head of it reached the mysterious cable-hole. At that the mate gave a signal and stopped the winch. Then a very interesting thing happened:

The Voyage of the Norman D.

They dragged the great cat block (a block and tackle attached near the crosstrees of the foremast) over to the side of the ship, slipped around the tail of the anchor a great hook with a link in the end of it, and caught the hook of the cat block into that link. The tackle was wound around the winch, which was again started, and thus the tail of the anchor was lifted up until the upper fluke slid into place in the anchor plate. There it was made fast, and that operation was over.

WHEN we had dropped anchor we had not taken down the sails — they could hardly be any trouble in such a calm — and we got under way again easily and quickly. Now, for the first time, on looking down into the water beside the ship, I noticed huge herds of what the crew called "sunfish" — really a kind of jellyfish. I can give no better description of them than that they looked a good deal like exceptionally juicy and delicious fried eggs, each with a round orange or yellow lump in the center, surrounded by a fancy frill of whitish. But they had what fried eggs have not: long and very elegant *tails*, bunches of long, long streamers, waving behind them, whitish in color, very narrow and very numerous — perhaps fifteen or twenty trailing behind one fried egg. These streamers are waved about in a curious way, and the white of the egg, also, is expanded and then contracted like a mysterious umbrella opening and shutting.

They drifted along in great shoals and herds, seemingly unable to move except by the motion of the waves and tides. I had a great deal of pleasure in watching them. I leaned over the side of the ship and gazed and gazed at them. I so far forgot my dizziness that I almost began to hanker for some nice, juicy, delicious fried eggs. Those jellyfish made my mouth actually water. Every single one of them was slightly different from every other. At first they seemed all alike, but after you had watched them closely for a while you could see the differences right off. To begin with, there was a great variation in size. Some were as much as eight inches in diameter when spread out, others no more than three. Some looked as though they had been off to war, and appeared rather ragged and shabby. And then there was a great variation in color, in brilliance. The white part was just about the same in all of them, except that some seemed to be much more elegantly and fancily frilled. But the yolk of the egg varied from pale yellow to a fiery scarlet. Some had small and insignificant yolks and very fine whites; others seemed nothing but yolk with a tiny edging, a frilled collar. The ones with both large yolks and fancy whites were, of course, the finest.

And these curious creatures certainly had expression in their faces. Some looked as though they were in a great hurry — as though they were gathering up their robes of state around them and hastening on; others were small, dainty, modest, and very scornful of the more splendid ones; some went sailing by, looking, for all the world, as though they were lost in a remote dream. These had far-away, vacant expressions. Others went by with an extremely haughty, self-conscious air; and some, usually the most gorgeous, drifted past with a bland smile of self-satisfaction. These fried-egg creatures certainly are a race by themselves, different from anything else on land or sea, and with their own characters and personalities. I am sure they have characters and personalities!

The wind was coming up slightly, and, though the roll was increasing steadily as we drew nearer to the open sea, we thought the sails didn't flap or the booms swing and groan quite so much as before. We had high hopes of getting out of the shoals by dark. We passed more and more lightships, and buoys of all kinds; and since we were now, on account of the changing tide and the high swell from the open sea, making leeway very fast, it was often quite tricky work to dodge them. Captain Avery took the wheel a good deal, and was constantly changing the sails, especially the important spanker, in order to get every bit of breeze — to get more steerageway on and diminish the leeway. This constant changing of the great spanker was quite a joke among the crew. I would say: "Why, it's a long time since you've done anything to the spanker!" and they would laugh. But I didn't want to appear as though I didn't know why they did this and that to the sails — as a matter of fact, I quite surprised myself with my comprehension of their tactics — and I hope I didn't overdo the matter.

WHEN it was almost dark we could see, not far ahead, the exit from the dreaded shoals, and beyond that the wild, free ocean, a gleam of gray-blue. When I looked off across our part of it, I could see how it heaved and throbbed. It was like watching a human heart beating. It seemed strange to look away over it, and, instead of seeing it steady, firm, fretted with ripples, to find it rising high and then mysteriously subsiding again — sinking back down. One could not distinguish between the swells, or even detect their summits or their valleys. Only, when I saw the sea rise near the side of the schooner, I would know that the schooner, too, would rise in an instant, and instinctively I learned to prepare myself for the rise, and then for the sinking into the hollow. In that way I began, gradually and painfully, to get my sea legs on, and with a little practice (which I took walking about the ship) I learned to walk in the midst of it without staggering and stumbling and clutching the taffrail too much. I would win the respect of the cook, yet! I didn't blame him in the least for being amused at the antics of a landlubber.

Our exit from the shoals was exciting. It was a difficult bit of navigation, especially in such a slight breeze, with so much swell and tide and leeway. Here the captain, in spite of his nervousness and his habit of becoming hectic if anything went the least wrong, showed his real skill. But we had a narrow escape if ever there was one. We looked ahead at the narrow opening, beyond which rose and fell the sea. What a sense of isolation and solitude! I know nothing comparable to it, except possibly being mist-bound, alone, on a mountain-top. It gives you just about the same spellbound feeling. And we weren't really out in the open sea yet: we could only see it, stretching away, boundless, ahead. Yet we were already beginning to feel the edges of that solitary spell, fanning our cheeks, as it were, and wrapping the little schooner in its fringes.

The exit was dotted with buoys and lightships. Whistling buoys droned and roared. Somehow the uncanny sound of them is like a knell bidding drowned mariners rise from the sea; and in the midst of that spell and that quiet I half expected to see ghosts rising, folded in their shrouds. The bell buoys are strange, too. Some of the bells are harsh and realistic, but others have a soft, mellow ring, like an unearthly deep church bell. Immediately they recalled to me the far-away church bells sounding through the sea from the above-world in Arnold's "Forsaken Merman."

The captain knows the passage of the shoals very thoroughly, and on which side to sail of every single buoy. He guided the *Norman D.* among them very deftly and surely, in spite of the adverse weather conditions.

Flocks of foam-white gulls swooped, uttering their uncanny cries. In spite of the amount which I wrote about sea gulls in *The House Without Windows*, I had never until now realized what their call is like. It is a shrill, shrill mew, like that of a cat

The Voyage of the Norman D.

when it cries faintly — a forlorn note to hear from a swift bird in flight.

Now we could see the huge surf booming on the sand bars at the exit, where the high swells would come pounding in, wholly different from the quiet, even monsters they are farther out. We could see the long crests of surf where the waves broke, then, champing, galloped up the bar and settled back once more. We were near enough to hear their roaring.

There was a large bell buoy just before the exit. We were to go to starboard of it. We headed as far to starboard as we could without sailing on the wrong side of other buoys. But not quite enough room was allowed for leeway. With the tide sweeping us down, we were washed toward that buoy alarmingly fast. The nearer we came, the huger and more sinister it looked, while the boom of its swinging bell became more and more like howling. Now it loomed like some dark red dragon from the midst of those mysterious swells. Every billow carried us toward it; the breeze failed us when we needed it most; we could see with half an eye that it was unlikely we should clear. Happily, the constant swinging and banging of the sails helped; at every roll, and every time they filled with a spurt, the schooner was carried on a little. But still we simply went skidding across the sea sideways. I believe we could have sailed to Nova Scotia quicker side-on than head-on! Faster and faster we glided toward the buoy, which became more and more uncanny as the high, round swells half buried it and then uncovered it again. Finally we were within six feet of it — and, on a forward roll, we cleared it, *just*; it slid mysteriously beneath our davits. A close shave! Probably, if we had hit it, it would have done us more damage than we did it. Those buoys are made to stand the wildest weather. They are strong, though rather unsteady monsters.

A few moments afterward we had slid neatly out the exit,

and were now in the open sea. There was no appreciable difference except that the roll was steadily increasing; the sea gave it more room to increase. Now that the hot sun of midday had set, the roll seemed only pleasant to me.

We turned in a good deal earlier that night; there was nothing in particular to stay up for. The roll was fairly heavy, and when I lay down in my hard bunk it was like sleeping in a treetop all night during a high wind, or in a cradle; but it was more delightful than a cradle, because we were riding upon the heart of the sea. It was strange to feel the roll so heavy that there was a strain on first one side and then the other, and if I relaxed entirely my head rocked from side to side.

In the morning I had to be waked up; the roll had made me sleep more soundly than I ever slept in my life. When I went on to the throbbing deck there was nothing but blue, blue ocean around me, stretching out to the thirty-two horizons; stretching away, a vast, boundless space — stretching away — away — forever. What isolation, what terrible isolation!

The weather conditions were monotonous all day. There was no wind — no wind at all — and one could not have told that we were moving. We were in the midst of space; we might have been marooned on the cold, desolate moon. Of course the sails flapped, the booms creaked; and somehow I felt myself trying to hold back that sound. It was as if I hardly dared breathe or speak myself; as though *nothing* should make a sound in the midst of the silence and the space that surrounded us. Oh! then was the sea like a living creature — cold, but with a mighty, throbbing heart. I was walking on the heart of the sea; I was sleeping on it; and I could always, night and day, feel it beating beneath my feet, or beneath my back. Or perhaps it was the life, the heart, of the ship that I felt. For now I knew that our schooner was superbly alive. She carried, amid the snow of her sails, a living heart and soul.

The Voyage of the Norman D.

* * *

MY shipmate was returning from a visit to the galley. I accosted him: "Well, how does the cook seem this morning?"

"Oh, the cook is getting wonderfully rabid! He talks about busting the captain's jaw — and not only his jaw, but his blankety-blank jaw. And holds he could do it, and would if a chance offered!"

Exciting! It looked as though a real mutiny might start at any moment now, with the cook as ringleader. I did so wish there would be a mutiny — a little of the piratical on this seemingly peaceful schooner! I went forward to have a yarn or two with him, hoping that I should get the edges of this sudden burst of violence. I was not in the least disappointed. Evidently the cook made no difference between ladies and anyone else; he went swearing right along. And I never could get over my surprise at the way he swore, his whole character seemed so very, very inconsistent. In appearance he was a delightful little old man, gentle and kind as a lamb, not hurting a fly. Yet, when you knew him, there was the most wonderful spark of temper, of pride, of malice. He had the sad face of an old monkey, and his apron strings flopped behind him, and he wore suspenders — but *how he could swear!* I used to think that I could feel the galley shake around me, and I felt that at any moment the ship might blow up or burst into flames.

"Well, mate," said I, when I approached him, "good morning to you!"

"Good morning." A deep sigh; profound silence. He was sitting in the galley door, as usual, with his back against the starboard side of the doorway. He was smoking, and looking altogether so harmless and peaceful!

"Well," said I, "and how's life treating you, mate?"

"Oh, Lordy, Lordy," said he. "Captain Avery — I'd like to bust his mildewed old jaw for him — and I could do it, too!"

Apparently he was repeating exactly what he had said before. How delightful to get this explosion from that embodiment of all peacefulness!

"Why, what's the matter, steward? What's the skipper done to you now?"

"Well, he says he don't like my grub. How kin he expect any man to cook when there's nothing to cook with? Now, look a' this old stove, and this rotten old oven. Why, when I bake my bread, I've got to keep it in hours longer than it ought to be in, in order to get it done at all. I haven't a drop of flavoring extract on board this ship; I haven't a bit of anything to make nice things out of; I can't make cakes, I can't make good pastry with what I've got here; I have no jams or jellies of any kind — how can he expect me to do any cooking for him? That's what I'd like to know!"

And again this sad little old man seemed to sink down into himself.

ALL day long I walked around the decks, talking to the sailors, spinning yarns with Bill and Bob, and even with Captain Avery. We felt, to be sure, a little distant from the skipper. His attitude suggested that he was getting tired of his passengers. He always seemed to draw off by himself in a corner of the deck; or he would study his charts, down in the dark of the cabin, spreading them out flat on the floor, and getting down on top of them on his knees and elbows; or else he would come around and interfere in other persons' conversation, by saying "Hey?" in the middle of sentences not addressed to him at all. Sometimes he would come around where we were talking and "jine in" very freely, without asking permission. Then, of course, the conversation would be entirely transferred to his side; for when he got going there was no hope for anyone else to talk unless, by mistake, the old man asked a question. On and on he would go, taking up the talk just where we had left off, and continuing it in his own way, strangely distorting it. Moreover, we began to see truth as well as exaggeration in the cook's statements. We had begun, too, to become more interested in the crew than in the skipper. But, in spite of all this, the captain was the captain; and he was very amusing and entertaining as well as boring, if you looked at him in the right light.

Somehow, in spite of the calm and the tides, we were making headway. I didn't understand it at all — especially as the sails did nothing but flap and apparently carried us backwards as much as forwards. But the captain said we were off Cape Cod, though we didn't go in sight of it. There were a few jellyfish about; not nearly so many as there had been during our passage through the shoals, for apparently those queer creatures stick to the shallower water. I couldn't help wishing for a wind. But I was on a ship; and, after all, that was enough. Moreover, at this rate I had the prospect of being on a ship for several days to come. Here I was, leading the life I had madly wanted, living with the sailors, forming a companionship with them, gazing upon the expanse of the shuddering, boundless sea, watching the sails shaking above me — studying the tactics and the working of a *sailing* vessel.

And here I was, chinning in an extremely familiar way with my friend Mate Bill, who had somehow or other become quite intimate with me. I mocked him considerably about his "breeze-o'-wind." "Where's that 'breeze-o'-wind' you promised us, mate?" "Coming! You wait and see." The length of time which we could spend talking about that "breeze-o'-wind" was extraordinary. The mate maintained, more in joke than seriously, that there was going to be a northeast gale. And I laughed, not because I disagreed with him, for I believed him perfectly, but because it did seem so fantastic that this silence, this terrible calmness, could change into a ripping northeaster. The mate understood this feeling of mine perfectly. He chuckled his sly, mysterious, piratical chuckle and said that the wind was coming; he wouldn't be at all surprised if it came the next day, and he was sure it would come the day after that, at latest.

* * *

A TRIFLE more about our skipper. By this time we were winning the great favor of the crew, and especially of the mate, with whom both of us talked for hours at a stretch. The *Norman D.* badly needed a coat or two of paint. The skipper was most desirous to have the painting done during the voyage, and this very calm, lazy weather seemed the ideal time. Two or three of the crew were usually at work; also, my shipmate made the time go by painting. The captain's desire was to have the whole inside of the ship painted by the time we reached Bridgewater, but he seemed doubtful that it would be possible to do this. "You wait," said he to us — "you'll see how much painting there'll be done!" But Mate Bill would come over and say to me: "It's his own fault if we don't get the vessel painted by the time we get down to Nova Scotia. 'Cause we could do it perfectly well; a three-years' child could do it if only he could be let alone! But here's the old man bothering us and looking over our shoulders at every stroke. What does he know about painting? Lord! He paints worse than any of us. I tell you, if he had the chance he'd make one can of paint go for the whole vessel! He takes a brush, and dips it, and then daubs — a daub here, a daub there, and not enough anywheres. Look a' that bit of the taffrail he painted. A cat could do it better! Then, after he's done three inches of that, he goes forrard, daubing all the time, till he gits to the fo'c'sle; and then he puts a daub on that, and a daub on this!"

"I think, mate, it makes the cook mad to see him come forward at all."

"Certainly it does! It makes any sailor mad! What's he got to do forrard? That ain't his place. His place is aft, and I wish to brimstone he'd stay there. He ain't supposed to come off that poop deck. He ain't supposed to come no further 'n them steps. Forrard's *my* place — there's no sense in both of us there. 'N' if he comes forrard, I go aft. Forrard's my place. I'm supposed to do the work there, and see that the work gets done. The old man's supposed to tell me anything he wants done, and then I'm to see that it gets done. But I can't, and I lay 'tain't my fault. Why, anyone comin' aboard this vessel — if the owner come aboard and saw a little paint here, 'n' a little there, he'd ask the captain: 'Who's your mate aboard here?' 'N' the old man 'd say: 'Bill McLeod.' 'Well, he's a shockin' poor mate!' There, you see! all the blame gets round on to me again. If he'd only let us alone, we'd get the whole ship done. We'd get it done within three days, if this calm weather keeps up."

Bill was right. He had described the tactics of the "old man" perfectly. (He used to make a great to-do, Bill did, about that phrase, "old man." "I dunno why it is," he would say, "but I allus called any cap'n I ever had 'old man'; whether he's young or old, it's all the same — he's allus the 'old man.'")

"I don't think the cook cares much about Captain Avery."

"Oh, the cook hates him!" Again Bill chuckled, and his wicked black eyes twinkled. "He hates 'im like bitter p'ison!"

"I think it's very funny, the way Bob mocks at him so much."

"Yes, it's funny. But you get tired of it. Now, Bob is young, and he's awful fresh and careless; everythin's a game to him. He has a lot of fun mocking the old fellow that way. But I wouldn't do it; not me! One thing I was always taught, 'n' that was to respect people older 'n myself. Now Cap'n Avery's old, and he's a meddlin' old cat, but I niver sass him; not me! I've niver sassed him but once in me life, 'n' I've sailed with him a lot, too. I've sailed with him a lot, 'n' he's got to know me good, so he sometimes calls me Bill."

"When was it that you sassed him, mate?"

"Oh, that was a couple o' years ago, on another voyage I took with him."

"And what did Captain Avery do that made you sass him?"

"Well, it was in the evenin', and a terrible squall come up, and we had to get down the sails in a hurry. He orders us to take down the jibs first, and we was just gettin' the jibs down when somethin' went wrong with the tackle. The old man see what was the matter, and he come runnin' up forrard, giving orders and shouting. He was awful nervous. He allus was a nervous old cat. Well, somehow I didn't stop to think, and it made me kind of mad to see him come runnin' up forrard, shouting that way, and I sassed him back, 'n' I said: 'I wish to Beelzebub you'd get aft to your own place!' Well, the old man went. But a'terwards I see the tears runnin' down the poor old fellow's cheeks, he was so excited. Well, I niver, niver sassed him back again. But sometimes it riles me, the things he does. I think that's why he likes me, 'cause I am respec'ful to him. So it sometimes does rile me, the way Bob mocks him, and I talk to Bob a lot. But it niver does no good."

"And is Captain Avery a good man, supposing you get into a gale?"

"Oh, yes, he's a skillful old fellow. But anyone that's been to sea as long as he has *ought* to be skillful. He is clever and quick, but awful nervous, and he shouts and calls a lot. One good thing about Captain Avery is this: he has a good loud voice. You never have to come aft to ask what he says!" And Bill's eyes sparkled again.

"Do you think he ever has happened to hear when Bob mocks at him?"

"Well, I dunno. Bob does sometimes mock awful loud — but then, the old man is good and deef. But I wouldn't be at all surprised."

Indeed, Bob seemed to be growing steadily more daring. He used often to mock, even when the old man hadn't given an order, just for the sake of amusing the rest of the crew. It *was* amusing to hear the captain call the crew "boys." If he wanted anything done, it was always "Here, boys! Here, boys!" until someone came to execute his orders. (It rather disappointed me that he didn't call them "mates," or "my hearties," or "my bullies," in true piratical fashion. But one can't expect too much!) And Bob would stretch out his neck, and lift up his head like a bird about to sing, and screech, quite as loudly as the skipper himself: "Here, boys! Here, boys!" You could see his bronze throat quivering when he called, just like that of a bird. And then he would lower his head into himself and chuckle.

Bob was especially good-looking in a bright red sweater. He used to wear this sweater whenever it was the least bit chilly, and then he was usually so busy, or perhaps so lazy, that he never seemed to have a chance to take it off, even when it grew warm. Of him, more later.

During those calm days there was a great deal of warm weather. I went about, in my old blue shirt with a sailor collar and my old black pants, very gaily indeed, feeling sailorly and wanting to show the crew that I didn't put on airs or try to be superior to them. In fact, I admitted my inferiority by asking them questions about ropes, their names and uses. The ropes on a schooner are surely the most complicated things on earth, except those of a square-rigger, which both Mr. Rasmussen and our cook told me were a thousand times more complicated. As for the schooner, there was only about one rope which I could always be sure of — the foretopsail clew line. That particular rope had broken, and the mate had run in a brand-new one — a bright rope, white among the dark, weather-beaten, dirty ones. I could always tell it by a glance — until it began to get dirty, too.

Again we turned in early. We had discovered that it was really much simpler to do so, because we had neglected bringing a flashlight. There were no lights on the ship except lamps, and there was no lamp in the "bathroom," and consequently no way to find the water bucket without lighting a match. (I had overturned it two or three times in the rolling.) The ship's lamps, by the way, were arranged in little rings of brass which projected on arms from the wall, and as the ship rolled crazily the lamps, too, would swing about, but keeping themselves upright in the gimbals.

THE next day the weather conditions were annoyingly the same. There was no wind; there was nothing but that steady roll, which I now began to enjoy quite a lot, though it did wear on one. I would look up at the horizon as the bow of the ship plunged down, and I would see it away up in the sky above me somewhere. Then, as the bow swung back, the horizon would vanish beneath the forefoot of the schooner. When the bow swung down, how far above it we, on the poop deck, seemed! and then how formidably the bow would loom above us on the return roll!

I joked more than ever with Bill about his "breeze-o'-wind." But he only chuckled and told me that I wanted to get there too fast, and that we should have the wind yet, and plenty of it, too.

I would look out over the restless ocean and see where a tiny breath of air made blue ripples on the silver- gray, and I would nudge Bill and say: "Well, the breeze seems to be coming up a little now!" And Bill would reply: "Yes, we'll have that wind in no time now!" And the breath of air would die down, and again there would be nothing to break the monotony of the sea.

But, aside from the weather, the day turned out to be a remarkably exciting one for me. For one thing, I had been forbidden by my strict family to do anything whatsoever without the consent of Captain Avery. "Just because you're *not* told not to do anything," they said, "you're not to assume that you can do it. You have to *ask* first." "Oh, that's easily managed," I replied. I must ask every time I wanted to go up in the rigging (though, on account of my dizziness, I had not as yet gone up); I should certainly have to ask before going out on the jibboom; I should not be allowed to steer, even though I knew the points of the compass. The most I could do was to ask the names and uses of things. For this I usually sought out Mate Bill. When he was off duty, the two of us would sit together in some concealed corner behind the fo'c'sle, or on the fo'c'sle deck, or on the other side of the after deckhouse from where Captain Avery was at that time; and then we would have "a go of it." I would ask him questions, and he would take them seriously. He didn't joke over it, and he didn't laugh because I didn't know. He would say: "Now, I approve of answering questions that anyone asks me, if so I can. The steward here, he'd fool you half the time."

But I wanted my privileges! I decided that I would begin to acquire them again. I climbed up on the spanker boom often; I had been told that that was all right. I used to walk out on it, leaning against the sail and walking on the windward side of it, until I came almost to where the boom overhung the water. Then, feeling a slight disgust at the strictness of everything, I would stop. Of course I could do this only when the breeze held the sails steady. (Two or three times during that day this happened.) Otherwise I should be flapped off the boom. I used to go by myself on the fo'c'sle deck a good deal, and I would climb around and sit on the forward capstan or on the staysail boom or on the very forward part of the bow, as near the tip as I could. Then I would have a longing upon me to go out on the jibboom. But when I saw those frail footropes, overhanging the open sea itself, and the whole jibboom waving up and down, I decided that, even if I were given permission, it was a little precarious for me. But I said I should come around to it sooner or later — and, after all, it was only my first voyage — and, after all, I could climb better than Richardson — and, after all, I was really doing very well for such an amateur!

I did long to steer, though. How I wished someone would give me a hint or two! I was a little worried about asking anyone save my friend the mate. I resolved that, sometime when he had the wheel, I would ask him. But I found that the mate, because of his rank, hardly ever took the wheel. Sometimes he would take it for a while, during Bob's trick, so that Bob could go down to dinner; that would be after he had had his own. But I had an itch on me to steer that day. It was after dinner when I felt the itch; they were constantly tampering with the sails, and it was, as usual, Bob's trick (it seemed to me as though it were almost always Bob's trick), and Bob had just left the wheel to help close-haul the spanker. I came walking slowly aft at that moment, and Bob called out to me: "Here, take the wheel while I fix this bally sail."

To be requested to steer!

"Do you know the points?" he shouted.

"Yes!"

"East by north."

"East by north, bo's'n!"

A moment afterwards I had picked out the point, and, with the feeling of those hand-worn wooden spokes in my palms, I guided the lubber line about and kept the schooner at east by north. I found it was not so hard; I could really do it! The only thing about it that puzzled me was that, when the ship swung off her course by a tiny eighth of a point, it took a very generous motion of the tiller to bring her back. But oh, how like a sailor I felt! And when Bob left close-hauling the sail, with Roy to help him, and came back to his trick, and saw that the lubber line was still on the dot of east by north, he certainly was pleased. He said: "I'll have to stand with you, 'cause if I don't the old man won't like it. But you'll get to steer good before long. Now I'm going to do something up forrard. If the old man asks you why you're steerin', you tell him I said you could."

"Can you trust me with her all right?"

"Oh, sure! You're gettin' to steer good!"

Well, the old man didn't happen to pass by at that particular moment — perhaps he was down in the cabin — but I certainly did feel a huge sense of responsibility. There I stood, holding the ship to her course very neatly. And, though it took all my concentration at first to keep that tiny black line on that tiny black point, I grew more and more used to it, and before long I got so that I didn't mind it at all. The bo's'n came back after a little and looked anxiously at the compass in the binnacle. But it was still all right, and he grinned. Presently the old man really did come by, and he saw that I had the wheel all to myself, and that Bob was standing doing nothing behind me, but watching like a cat. He, too, looked at the compass, and then at me, and then at the compass again. I grinned at him. He looked rather anxiously at Bob, and I heard him whisper: "Don't let her keep it too long. Do look out for her!" And then I heard Bob's careless voice reply: "Oh, sure! *She's* all right. She steers better than Richardson now." But, evidently to please the captain, he took the wheel, too. It was companionable to steer with another; yet I liked the feeling of having it alone. I steered more and more accurately all the time, and I got so that I could see when the schooner was about to slide off her point, and would head her off with the wheel.

I had the wheel for the second half of Bob's trick, and for the first half of Roy's. That made a whole trick; and the time went like foam. But toward the end of that time my eyes, unused to the strain, grew rather blurred. I could no longer see the line or the point very well, and, afraid of mistakes, I stopped. But I was becoming a sailor! My first voyage, and here I was "jining in" with the crew and the work like anything!

* * *

THAT morning, before the steering, I had had a rather amusing and exciting experience. The breeze seemed to be coming up a little, but it was just a whim. The sails were steady for a moment, and the captain wanted the spanker close-hauled. They were always doing something or other with that spanker; I never knew anything like it. Well, the captain decided, there was such a very light breeze, that he could do it himself. He loosed the sheet from the belaying pin on the starboard side of the schooner, leaving only one turn of the rope around the pin, and began to haul, letting all the strain go on to the pin — the true nautical way of close-hauling a sail when you want to do it alone. But the captain, as Bill often said, was "weaker 'n a cat," and to see him leaning back on the rope, clasping his horny hands around it desperately, and yet with the strength of that mighty sail all the time pulling him back toward the belaying pin, was comical. He raised his head, and I could see that at any moment he would begin his call of "Here, boys! Here, boys! Here, boys!" I wanted to be helpful as a sailor, and I immediately took hold of the sheet above the belaying pin and hauled and hauled, with the desperate strength which I always had when I wanted to be sailor-like, or wanted to show the crew and the skipper that I was sailor-like. I hauled while Captain Avery took up the slack which I made, by hauling it taut around the belaying pin. The two of us could just hold the sail and close-haul it half-inch by half-inch; but we weren't making very rapid progress, and the skipper was getting tired of it. And, after all and after all, he began to sing out: "Here, boys! Here, boys! Here, boys!" The bo's'n came aft in a bound or two, and, with a look of disgust at me to show that he was sick of that infernal "Here, boys!" he, too, began to haul. He took the sheet close under the block, I took it a little farther down, and the captain still stood on the other side of the belaying pin, making frantic gestures and taking up the slack. But evidently the sheet had been working towards the top of the belaying pin, for in a little spurt of wind it crept up to the top and over. The captain started shouting. The boom was too much for Bob and me without that extra turn around the pin, and both Bob and I were dragged rapidly, roughly, and resistingly across the deck. We went fast, because of the savage pull of the boom, but I had time to think quite a lot. I thought that it would pull me overboard; I thought of letting go; then I thought that I *mustn't* let go, I must just hang on like grim death and show them that I was sailorly. I felt myself come into a bit too sudden contact with the after capstan, and heard the bo's'n say "Let go, quick!" Then I saw that he had let go. And, next, everything was a blurred whirling. At last, as I neared the port taffrail, I let go, and the boom went wandering gently out until it was at right angles to the rail. I fell on my knees just against the rail; then, in spite of my jarring encounter with that capstan, I got up briskly and laughed. With Roy helping, all of us hauled the boom in again and made it fast.

* * *

IN the afternoon the crew, having less than nothing to do, all gathered on deck, sitting on hatches between the poop and the fo'c'sle, in the sun of the mid-afternoon, to talk. They all came out with the exception of Richardson and another Bill — an Irish Bill. There were the mate, the bo's'n, Roy, the cook, and I. It was the first time the crew had really shown signs of being friendly with one another. Not that they had quarrelled, but they never seemed to have anything much to say; they were gloomy and silent.

We carried a spare gaff on the starboard side, under the bulwarks 'way forrard. It seemed to be a favorite place to sit. The mate and I sat down on this gaff, side by side, while the bo's'n and Roy, who seemed to be great pals, sat on a forward hatch-cover, facing us. I began joking Bill about his "breeze-o'-wind." "When *is* it coming, mate?" said I. "Oh, sometime next month!" "We'll have to publish that," said I — " 'Bill predicts a breeze-o'-wind for next month.' " "But you wait," says Bill. "It's a-comin' yet, sometime tomorrow!" "That's far better," said I.

Then I subsided entirely and let the crew rattle on in their own way. Richardson had now come out of the fo'c'sle and was very feebly and painstakingly splitting up pieces of wood with the steward's little hatchet. He was doing it slowly, though neatly, and it looked as though he were not accustomed to it. The mate saw him, and I could tell at once, by the way his black eyes began to sparkle so maliciously, that he was going to say something to Richardson. And he said, in that solemn way of his, yet with a downward twist to the corners of his mouth: "Hey, Dick, don't hurry too much over that!" Richardson is very pleasant, no matter what is said to him, and he replied only with chuckles — rather gloomy ones. Then he fell to work sawing up some boards which had been left over from the lumber cargo; he brought out a small sawhorse and a saw and fell to work. But it went no better. Every stroke seemed to be painful, and he made very slow progress. Again the mate struck in, and said: "Don't kill yourself over that, Dick!"

The mate began to tell about various incidents of his career, which seems, on the whole, to have been a fairly interesting one. He has stuck to the sea for fifteen years, with hankerings now and then to do landsman's work, but always sooner or later returning to sailor life. He said: "Once they wanted me to go as mate on a schooner, fer seventy a month. I was workin' ashore then, an' I didn't want to go. But I was wanted badly enough — somehow, it seems I never had no trouble gettin' a berth as mate —"

"Well, no wonder," interposed Richardson from his sawhorse. "If you resigned up there at Bridgewater, I would too, by heaven! I wouldn't stand bein' hazed by the old man; not I! Why, Bill, it's you as keeps this crew together at all."

"Well," continued Bill (it seems customary for them to begin everything with a "well"; even I do it, more or less), "the owner of that vessel offered me seventy-five. But 'twas no better. I didn't want to go. I said I wouldn't, no matter how much he give me. 'Not for eighty?' says he. 'No, sir!' says I. 'Eighty-five?' 'No,' says I, ''n' you might as well make up your mind to it, sir! I'm not goin' to do a sailor's work no more.' 'Wouldn't you go fer ninety, Bill?' 'No. Don't you coax no more. I'm not goin'!' But he kep' on arguin', and he riz five dollars every time he opened his mouth, and, by thunder, I went, fer a hundred and ten. That's how bad I'm wanted! And here I am with Cap'n Avery, fer sixty flat, and a row over that, too!"

The cook had now come out of his galley, and he stood listening, his apron tied behind him, and a curious expression of scorn and disdain on his face. Said he: "You think ye're so badly off, don't you? Why, when I used to sail in the old square-riggers, we used to get thirteen dollars a month, flat — no more. And the mate — he didn't get no more than seventeen. You think the work is so awful hard here, don't you? Why, listen to me! Every single morning all hands was called on deck at four o'clock; some ships had it half-past three. Then we had to wash, and scrub, and sooge[1], and sand, and holystone, and squeegee the decks, forrard and aft. 'N' when that was done we had to go aloft and polish up all the brass work, 'n' the brass along the bulwarks, and the cook had to polish his kids and pans, and put them in the front of the galley for the old man to examine when he come forrard in the morning. It took till breakfast t' get all that done. Why, you sluggards would take all day over the work that we used t' do in an hour! And do you know what? Listen to me — "

But here an interruption came in the shape of an incident which made the crew laugh a great deal. The cook decided that he would come and mingle with us; he would sit on the gaff and swing his legs around, and be chummy. So he walked robustly over to the spare gaff, his hands up under his apron in front. But somehow or other, nimble though the little man is, he missed his aim, as it were, and, instead of sitting on the gaff, he sat down *behind* it, with his knees over it. By that small miscue the dignity of the little old cook was suddenly spilled, turned upside down. But he pulled himself together again, hitched forward on to the gaff, blinking in the sun, and rocked himself back and forth. Then he began again where he had left off:

"Listen to me a minute. You talked about being hazed by the old man: you listen, and if you call this hazin', what you're havin', I eat rats fer dinner! When our old man used to come on deck, at eight bells, after everythin' aboard was all fixed up tidy as tidy, 'n' the deck holystoned 'ntil it was white as chalk all over, he used to bring his glass and come forrard and look away up at the riggin', t' see 'f the brass work was shining enough.

And if we hadn't polished it to suit him, he would make us go up aloft and do it all over agin."

All this time the cook had an imaginary glass in his hand, and was peering aloft through it, to see if the brass work were polished. He would peer and peer up at the mizzen-mast, and peer and peer at the mainmast, and then peer and peer indefinitely at the foremast. And very queer he looked, peering and peering that way through his imaginary glass.

" 'N' then," he went on, "after he had looked at that a while, he would come to the door of the galley and look at all the cook's tin pans and kids, that was spread out in the sun. 'N' if *they* wasn't polished to suit him, they would have t' be done over, 'n' the cook would get a good callin' down, too. — Fer the love o' Mike, what you laughin' at, bo's'n?"

The bo's'n had been chuckling and giggling, and now he was absolutely bursting with restrained merriment. "I was thinkin'," said he, "someone ought to have put pepper in the old man's eyeglass. Then, when he come along and tipped it 'way back to look up, he'd go around howlin' and howlin' and stampin' and swearin', and be a fine show — and then, if the fust mate ast him what was the matter, he wouldn't dare say, 'n' he'd say that the brass was polished so poor it made him curse!" The bo's'n delivered this strange harangue in the craziest voice you ever heard in your life, all the time chuckling as though about to burst.

"Well," returned the cook, vehemently, yet very solemnly — "I guess you nor no one else, neither, would dare to do anythin' like that. He'd regret it all his life, let me tell you! And you wouldn't do anything about the grub, neither. I suppose all you fellows think you're in a awful bad way with food. Do you want me to tell you what *we* used to have to live on? We had salt pork 'n' hard tack. 'N' that's about all. We used to have what we called 'duff' on Sundays, but that wasn't so good as the grub you have all the time. And they didn't even have potaters! Now, you shrimps git potaters all the time. Then, they on'y had 'em aft! Once we had a great hunk o' salt beef. It got all soaked up with salt water, but the cook made us eat it. It was hard as a rock, 'n' it lasted fer days and days, 'cause no one would eat it. 'N' it kept cropping up, and cropping up, and we couldn't get rid of it nohow. But we had to keep on chewin' it ('n' it was jist like leather), 'ntil every bit of it was gone. Why, we used to have food that cats and dogs wouldn't 'a' touched, 'n' that turkey-buzzards wouldn't 'a' picked up."

"Well!" said the bo's'n, in a voice of careless scorn, "blamed if I'd eat it, if 'twas as bad as all that."

"Now, my young man," said the cook, very severely, "you'd do exactly what everyone else did, you would."

"Wither me if I would! I'd fire it overboard. Why didn't you fire it overboard?"

"It was different then," said the cook — "very different. Sailors couldn't get fresh and flip then, by thunder. Why, every man of them would be fired and flogged, if they did that."

"Well," said the bo's'n, "why didn't they come aft and complain? Strikes me it ain't up to them to eat what's fit for hounds."

"Of course it wasn't up to them!" said the cook, "but they had to do 't all the same. I tell you, sailors weren't treated as men at all, then; they weren't so good as dogs! You think ye're so hard off, don't you? I'd like to have seen you in them times. Yes, by thunder, I would!"

"Well, but," said the bo's'n, whose careless brain was still working on the meat, "I'd take it out of the fo'c'sle with me, a little piece at a time, every time it come round — and then, when the old man or the steward wasn't around, I'd fire it over. That's what I'd do."

"No you wouldn't. You'd do what everyone else did — eat it 'ntil it was gone!"

"Well now," I interposed, "I think the bo's'n made an intelligent remark then. It would have been simple enough to do that — a little piece at a time." "Sure it would!" said the bo's'n, evidently glad to have someone agree with him. " 'Twould be the easiest thing in the world. I'm surprised none o' you thought of it."

"Huh!" said the cook — and that was all of that subject.

"Speakin' o' dogs and cats," said the mate, evidently deciding that it was about his turn — "once I was second mate in a schooner, 'n' the old man had a cat. He was fond o' that animal, I tell you! But the boys, they got kind o' mischievous 'bout it 'n' decided they'd play a trick on the skipper and get rid o' that cat. So, one time when we was gettin' a tug out o' the harbor, one o' the boys picked up the cat by the tail and threw him down into the tug. Gee! I'll niver ferget how surprised the boys in the tug looked, to see a cat come flyin' down. An' I'll niver ferget the skipper. He didn't know what had happened to the beast; he niver did know. 'Cause he'd 'a' been powerful mad if he'd found out — but he niver did find out what happened to his cat."

There was a silence, as the old man emerged from the cabin door, walked over to the port taffrail, and peered over at us, with a strange look of meddlesome curiosity on his visage, and an ugly, trembling glare. Everyone looked at him, and the bo's'n said: "Here, boys! Here, boys! Here, boys!" in his mocking voice. "You wait!" he added. "He'll be hollering in a minute." As a matter of fact, the skipper didn't start calling; he only looked forrard as though he would like to eat us. I suppose it enraged him to see me preferring the crew's company to his; and perhaps it also enraged him to see the crew lying all over the deck, so " 'xcruciating idle." Then he went to see about the steering.

"Well," began the mate, "last night I tried again to beat the points of the compass into Richardson's head." This was to me, the crew having dispersed momentarily. "But he can't learn, and he won't learn. I never seen a dumber lad."

"He can't box the compass, mate?"

"Indeed he can't! He can't remember them points for a minute. And he does make the dumbest mistakes, too. Why, early this mornin', when 'twas his trick, he almost steered us right into a small fisherman crossin' our bow. The boat got swept towards us, on account o' leeway, and Richardson held us right to our course 'n' didn't know enough to heave to. And the lad was goin' t' keep right on goin' 'ntil we hit the fisherman, but I see what was happenin', and I come aft and took the wheel out of his hands and hove us to. But he's dumb!"

"I'm getting so I can steer pretty easily, mate." "Oh, you can steer good. A few more tries at it, and you'll be steerin' as good as anybody. You steer a good sight better 'n Dick, now."

How I did love the mate's flattery of my seamanship!

At this point something occurred which sent a mighty roar of laughter from the crew and gathered them together again for more yarns. Richardson had been steering for a long time. Most of his trick was over, and he was listening impatiently for the welcome sound of eight bells from the ship's clock below. The clock struck after a few seconds — seven bells. But Richardson was so elated with the idea that his trick was over, and that the watch would now be changed, that he never stopped to wait until the bells had finished striking; he took it for granted that it was eight, and pulled the cord of the after bell (on the deckhouse just over the binnacle, within reach of the helmsman) eight times. First the crew looked puzzled, and then, amid shouts of laughter, Bob yelled out: "Hey there,

Dick! What you strikin'?" Richardson looked foolish for a moment. But he quickly recovered his good nature, and said, blushing: "Wasn't that eight bells?" This time the crew was too convulsed to reply. Only the cook remained solemn. He gave one disgusted look from the galley door. He felt that it was altogether beneath his dignity to laugh. *He* wouldn't condescend even to smile.

The boys were now back again, sprawled over the hatchways and the deck. But the cook, evidently rather disgusted, as always, with the freshness and the greenness of our crew, went back into his galley, muttering: "Oh, Lordy, Lordy!" and we didn't see him again that afternoon.

The conversation of the crew changed to an extraordinary subject: teeth. (I won't repeat all the gory, gory details.) The mate began by saying: "Well, I think when I get to Bridgewater, I'll have all my teeth pulled out, and get me a set of false ones."

"Well," said the bo's'n, "I imagine that would be a good plan. Does it hurt?"

"What do you want to know for?"

"Well, I think some day I'll do the same. Is 't 'xpensive?"

"Some is and some isn't. A couple o' years ago I wanted to have a tooth pulled out, and I see in the paper where a dentist pulled teeth fer twenty-five cents apiece. So I says: 'That's the place fer you, Bill,' 'n' off I went. Well, when I got there, I had a tooth pulled. 'How much is it?' says I. 'Fifty cents,' says he. 'But I see in the paper where you pull teeth fer a quarter!' 'So I do,' says he, 'when you have more than one pulled. Fifty cents fer one. A quarter fer each tooth, if you have more than one pulled.' 'All right,' says I, 'go ahead!' And he went on pullin' and pullin', and he took out nine teeth. I've only got seven in my upper jaw now."

"But," said the bo's'n, "does it hoit?"

"No."

"Well, I've got a couple o' teeth that I'll have pulled. What do you say we go somewheres in Bridgewater?"

"All right with me," said mate.

"You have yours pulled first, and see if it hoits, and then I'll have mine pulled."

"Agreed."

"And say, Roy," went on the bo's'n, "if you'll pay fer mine I'll have three pulled."

"Agreed," replied Roy, and that was the end of that. I was rather glad. Enough is enough.

THROUGH the rest of that day the weather was monotonous, but very beautiful. The sea heaved and throbbed endlessly — dappled waves of silver-gray, constantly shifting shadows, pools of dark blue. The sky was clear all day, and the weather was very warm — in fact, uncomfortably so during the early afternoon. The sails stayed white with sunlight, and there were always sun-sparkles on the sea. Of course I had to have my little joke with Bill about the "breeze-o'-wind." He said that if it didn't come tomorrow he would never attempt a weather-prophecy again, but that he was almost sure it would come.

And that leads me to say more of Bill. He is the best of mates; at least, in these modern times. In the days of the old clippers he would have needed a great deal of hardening down before he would be acceptable as an officer. But now he is just about as perfect as the mate of a lumber schooner could be. He is unutterably patient, and more willing to work than the men before the mast. In fact, he has a paintbrush in his hand as much as anyone. Of course this attitude — especially his willingness to do small jobs about the deck — wins the crew to him. You remember what Richardson said about his holding the crew together? Well, that's a fact; he does. They were all dissatisfied with Captain Avery; if it weren't for Mate Bill, they would certainly resign. And his willingness to work keeps them at work. None of his orders are slighted — except possibly by Bob, the bo's'n, who, being his brother, is naturally very careless.

I asked Bill if he didn't like to have Bob for his bo's'n. He replied that it was nice in some ways to sail with part of the family, but that at the same time he wished that Bob weren't the bo's'n, but only a man before the mast, because, being his brother, he was often careless about important orders. And the mate said that Bob often used to sass him back. "Once," he said, "just the other day, I ast Bob to get to work painting the bulwarks, and I give him the can and the paintbrush and everything. Then Bob says: 'Aw, drop yerself overboard! I've done enough paintin' t'day!' Well, I didn't say nothing; I jist turned around and left him. If I'd done what I ought to have done, I would have heaved him overboard. But I'm not made that way — I have a tender heart. And that's the trouble with me as a mate: I'm not hard enough."

Bill had pronounced his one fault — tenderheartedness. But when I looked at him, so brawny, and strong, and brown, and piratical, it seemed rather ridiculous to define him of all persons as tenderhearted. I should rather have liked to see him heave Bob overboard — and then hoist him on deck again by the throat halyards! I imagine that the mate really did have hard times getting things done, with Bob as bo's'n. Bill used to say that any of the rest of the crew, even Richardson, would probably have made a better bo's'n than Bob; though Bob was all right, he said, when he didn't have Bill for mate.

* * *

BILL'S weather-prophecies, however belated their fulfillment may be, certainly are *true*, and no joke. When I went on deck the next (and fifth) morning, after a hard sleep and another waking-up by force, the sea was agitated, the sails were full and steady, and the proud *Norman D.* was leaning a very little. The man at the helm seemed to have an easier time of it, now that steerageway was on her. And the whole atmosphere of everything had changed somewhat. Instead of the gloomy, drowsy atmosphere, everything was gay, alert, alive. And yet the sea was not really boisterous, either — only playful and laughing. The sun was out brilliantly, and the whitecapped waves danced. I could feel the wind all through me, and the sails could feel it, and the schooner loved it — loved it. It was not yet so strong as it had been for that short time on the afternoon of the first day; but as it came up, I could feel the schooner leaning more and more, and, though still it was only a playful breeze, there was something ominous in the sound of it. The waves pounded the side of the ship, breaking and breaking; the wings of foam rushed and roared, louder and louder. And then — what did I hear aloft? It was a gentle, high, shrill singing — an unearthly, indescribable sound which for a moment I could not identify. Then I knew: it was the song of the wind through the sails.

For long I have read and heard about that magic sound; but I was beginning to think that it was just part of the poet's imagination, and that he really meant the dashing of the foam or other sea noises. But no, it is quite true: the wind seeps out between the threads of the sailcloth and sings and sings, and the sound grows louder and more magical as the wind rises. This was sailing, as I had always dreamed of it.

Early in the morning we passed the loveliest small schooner I have ever seen, a small fisherman. She could not have been more than half our size, but in every detail she was as perfect as we. She carried foresail, mainsail, staysail, jib, and flying jib, and those long, pointed sails stretched out in front, full of wind, looked like the white wings of sea gulls. Keeled over on the port tack, she passed close under our stern. We could see the white bone she had in her small white teeth, and we could see that beautiful roundness of full sails. A sea gull — a white albatross sailing by — or, simply, a whitecap upon the waves!

We were off Cape Sable, the most southerly point of Nova Scotia. All day long the breeze rose, keeling us over more and more. The sails were watched as a cat watches a bird, in case a sudden squall should necessitate letting them out, or even reefing them. How I wished that we might have to reef!

The sea rose and rose in all its foaming greenness, until it had reached the point where it had been on the first day; but it did not stop there. It kept on coming up until, to me, it began to look actually raging. When night shut down, the sea was in a tumult; and the effect of the darkness on that raging water seemed to me to intensify its anger. When, for the first time, we ate with table racks, it was marvellously exciting. On previous days there had been enough roll to slop the tea about considerably; but the cook seemed to think that this long, steady, deep cant needed the racks more than a crazy rolling.

Bill thought the worst wasn't over yet; and since the seas were still becoming angrier and angrier, I believed him, and hoped that it was true. That night I went to sleep in a crazily tilted bunk. I slept as soundly as ever, and had to have another waking in the morning.

I consider that fifth day, the first of wind, as the beginning of the second half of the trip. Somehow, things changed on that day, and we began to see everything in a brighter, even a more piratical light.

I forgot to say that on that day we had seen our first black-fish. Bob was at the wheel, and his keen sailor's eyes had made out the fountain which, like whales, they blow up. This fish was near the schooner, and playing leisurely about, always blowing. Every now and then we would see its black, shiny back looming up out of the sea like a dark boulder, or the forked, Y-shaped tail. The water which it spouted was so like a whitecap, or a wave throwing up foam, that I didn't see it nearly so many times as the trained eyes of Bob.

* * *

IN the way of weather, the next day was without doubt the most exciting of the whole glorious trip. There was not so much talk with the crew, but the weather quite made up for that, and it, after all, was the greatest thing. When I woke up I had a sudden fancy that the ship had turned over, and was sailing upside down. Indeed, when I put my feet on the floor, it slid out from under me, as it were, and I had to be thoroughly awake before I could stand up, even dizzily. The leeward rail was almost buried, and later I discovered the sea spraying in through the scuppers.

When I thrust my head out of the cabin door, I was immediately blinded by the force of the wind, and I couldn't hear my own thoughts for the howling and rushing. A marvellous summer gale, dead from the northeast. Then I thought of Bill. It was just as he had said. I would never doubt or make light of his prophecies again. The sea was a raging wild whirlpool. The great green waves burst up and up, crested with roaring foam, breaking and breaking against the side of the ship, throwing their foam on to the deck. To me it seemed a typhoon. To them it was a summer gale.

I cannot describe the awesome howling and raging of it. The sea swirled wildly, dark green, foaming. The sky was overcast, and that made everything seem more sinister. The sails were close-hauled, but not yet reefed; we were on the starboard tack, and making ten knots — a very satisfactory speed. And I heard again that singing sound aloft in the sails, still more loud and unearthly than the day before.

The sea was nothing but a mad rush of flying foam. Everything seemed one with it — even the wind, even the *Norman D.* herself. Two storm petrels — Mother Carey's chickens — were blown like clots of dark foam across the sea; they had long, slender, dark wings, and they held them motionless and were scudded across. How I should have loved to see an albatross! Or a whale!

I could barely turn my face to the wind, and this fact helped to create my awed impression of it. When I wanted to walk forward I had to lower my head and hand myself step by step along the deckhouse, staggering even then. I saw some of the crew floundering. But the cook — not he! He walked in a straight, sure, steady line from the galley aft, with his heavy basket of food. When I asked Mate Bill whether this was a breeze, or a wind, or a gale, he said that it was "blowin' real hard. Yes, it sure is. Any more than this would be uncomfortable — we might have to reef." And the captain didn't scorn this either. At breakfast-time, when the table racks were up, the table set, and the bell rung, he came down into the cabin, his white hair blown with the wind, his cheeks fresh and rosy, and said: "Say, folks, it's blowin' quite a few up there!" It was. The only one who scorned that wind was — you couldn't guess. No, not with a hundred guesses! It was Richardson. *Richardson!* I asked him, just to compare a sailor's notion of this with a landsman's, whether he thought it was breeze, wind, or gale. And Richardson said: "Oh, I'd call this a little breeze." And it was not a joke! He was in dead earnest. He just wanted terribly to impress me.

When again I stuck my head out into that howling, again I

was awed speechless. The schooner now had her cutwater buried in foam. The roaring mountains of it which we piled up left her traces for miles upon the sea. I wish we could have seen her from farther off, as she leaned there, like a sea gull flying, or a wisp of foam. Now the sails were no longer so gently, evenly full of wind: they were stretched and puffed out furiously, distorted by the strain into unnatural shapes. I could see, looking at the canvas, how they were tugging at every squall.

The only place I could think of to sit down on was the canted leeward side of the deckhouse. I sat on the very edge of it, with my feet braced firmly against the taffrail. If that part of the rail had gone, I should have gone with it. But the old man came along, found me sitting there, and decided that I shouldn't be allowed to do *that* any longer. He told me that it was dangerous, and that I must get down. Down I got. Then I decided that I would go up on the fo'c'sle deck, and I asked Bill if that were all right. Bill replied that I oughtn't to do that, because the jib sheets were rather old and frayed, and with that strain on them might give way at any moment, sending the blocks banging about. He told me that he knew a man who had gone forrard on a job in the middle of a gale, and a jib sheet had given way, and he had been killed by a blow of the loose block. So I promised I wouldn't go there. Then all I could think of to keep myself warm was to run back and forth on deck, and since I couldn't do that aft, I went cautiously down the poop deck steps and started tearing like a race horse back and forth between the poop and the fo'c'sle, every now and then looking out the scupper holes or over the bulwarks at the foam. The waves were no longer great green hills crowned with their ivory castles: they were furious volcanoes. The sea was hurling aloft thousands of mountains, carving deep and terrifying valleys, and then ruthlessly destroying them again.

It was a curious and difficult experience to run upon the

deck. Besides the deep cant to leeward, the ship was rolling head-on, not on the waves of the gale, but simply on the tidal swell; and this roll seemed so much part of the cant that you didn't notice it until you began to have trouble managing your feet. It *seemed* as though the schooner were steady and firm. Yet, when you ran to the fo'c'sle, you were running first up a very steep hill which tired your legs dreadfully, then down so steep a hill that you almost fell on your face. Sometimes when I would put my foot down, the deck had slid out from beneath me and was 'way down at the bottom of the sea somewhere, and at the next step the deck was there long before I was, so that I would stumble over it, as it were.

When the cook saw me dashing so madly up and down the deck, he was amused, and shouted from the galley door: "What you doin'? Practisin' for a relay team?"

"Oh, just keeping warm," I replied.

"What do you think of the breeze?"

"Breeze!" said I. "I should rather call it a gale."

"Oh, yes," said he, "it's a pretty little wind for this time o' year. I didn't expect nothin' like this."

Again I was so awed by the sinister look of it that I could not speak. It was that way with me every time I looked at the overcast, gloomy sky, the raging sea, the strangely gleaming foam, the howling wind, the singing sails, the mountains of foam which we pushed up in great billows.

HOW the day went, I never did know; it went like the wind. Most of the time I was either running up and down the deck or standing on the poop deck, just gazing and gazing out to sea; or else I was watching the tactics of the *Norman D*. Of course, since the wind was coming from northeast, we had to tack. It was just as I had hoped, for I had always rather wanted to see how the schooner would tack in a good gale. I was disappointed, however, in the way she didn't lie close to the wind. She would run no nearer it than four points. The captain said that this was partly because she was light. "She's lightheaded," he explained; "that means she won't tack. She lay within three p'ints coming down, loaded." We would sail for some two hours on one tack; then the old man would take the wheel, in order to have all hands free for the sails. He would steer "by the wind" — that is, not taking any particular compass-line, but keeping an eye on the sails and sailing as near the wind as possible — and when everything was ready forward, he would roar out in his croaking, harsh old voice: "Ha-a-a-ard a-lee-e-e-ee!" And then the mate, usually on the fo'c'sle deck, would answer out in his more hearty voice: "Hard alee, sir!" And then you would be sure to hear the bo's'n, from some nook or cranny of the vessel, echoing: "Hard alee, sir!" The ship would swing over until she lay on the other side of the wind — though it always seemed as if the wind, not she, had changed. They tacked neatly, though a little frantically. But the cook disdained their performance, and spent a long time telling me how lazy and slow and ignorant they were, and how much more complicated it was to tack a square-rigged ship, when there were more than ten times as many sails and ropes, each one to be adjusted.

As I said, the day went very fast. There was nothing but the gale, the foam, the waves — now and then penetrated by one of the skipper's terrible whoops. (His voice seemed always on the point of cracking in two; he used to yell out that "Hard alee!" so loudly that his voice would vanish entirely into the air.) I shall never forget the strange, wild, melancholy feeling which that overcast and howling day gave me. I would sit for hours on the corner of the deckhouse, and watch it, and face up into it, and yield to it, and cower before it. It was even more sinister than mountain-tops with the wind droning about them; more so even than the night in which Daddy and I were on the top of Moosilauke — that night of the great gale, with the biting mist and the stinging sleet. We went out together that night, wrapped in blankets, braving it. I remember the mountain feeling which spellbound us, and the loneliness of it — and the way IT glowered at us out of the fog. This was like it. Every trace of that gay, piratical feeling left me. There was nothing but the gale. And, though it was all piratical and sailor-like, it crowded all feelings out of you except the feeling of its awesome self.

But the darkness, when it began to shut down, was the most overwhelming of all. To see the storm growing dark, and the foam still gleaming ghostlike, and to feel the wind howling in a way which it has at night — we almost trembled. The sailors didn't like it so well as we. They wished that it weren't from the northeast; anywhere but northeast! said they. The captain was heard to say something about anchoring, and the mate to say something about sailing a hundred miles that day without making an inch of progress to the northeast. While everything was vague rumor, and no one seemed to know much about anything, Bill came aft and was heard to say to the old man: "Are you going to anchor, sir?"

"Yes, I'm goin' t' get that mudhook down, Bill, if I can," said he. We made our way in pretty close to land somewhere off Cape Sable. Down with the sails, and down with the mudhook. And then, through the midst of the gale, with the howling above us all night, and the tossing of the ship, and the noise and confusion down in the cabin, we slept and rolled.

* * *

HERE I must say a little something about the captain's curious method of sleeping. We took two bunks aft, of course, and one of them had been the captain's. The skipper himself slept in the chart-room on an old couch, and he was always so sleepy when he went to bed for a snooze that he would tumble asleep with everything in the world piled on top of him. The afternoon of the first day, taking advantage of a chance to sleep a bit, he tumbled on to that couch, where we, innocently enough, had put a great deal of our luggage. We saw him sleeping there with bags of oranges, suitcases, and everything you ever heard of piled on top of him, as well as a tangle of blankets. Since then he had complained more or less about that couch, and how difficult it was to sleep on. It seemed to account for part of his decided nonchalance towards his passengers.

Our crude meals were getting to be terribly awkward now. There was a decided withdrawal from the captain, shared by everybody. The meals had their amusing aspects, though, and sometimes I would come near laughing aloud. The captain immediately started talking in his long-winded way about something which he didn't know the first thing about. The cook stood there, arms folded, glowering with solemn dignity, and the mate and I sat silently, now and then winking at each other. The only trouble was that we couldn't laugh aloud as we always wanted to.

Then there was the cook's feeling of superiority to the crew, in addition to his hatred of the skipper. There was a little sliding door which opened from the galley into the fo'c'sle — a door which the cook would open for a few seconds while he passed the crew's food through. He would pass the food through scornfully, as if throwing it to dogs. And then the way he would slam that little sliding door! a slam of pure disgust. Once, when a dish of mixed grub was sent through, our friend Richardson ventured to say mockingly: "What's that?" But it wouldn't pass with the cook; no indeed! He said, with a mild oath: "You'd better shut your jaw, or you won't get no more"; and *slam!* went the sliding door.

The cook showed in many ways what a real sailor he had been, and in what real sailing days he had lived. Sometimes, when three or four of the crew were struggling with some difficult job, clewing a topsail, close-hauling a sail in a breeze, or unfurling the topsails, he would come out, with his apron tucked up before him in a businesslike way, and with the strings always flopping behind, and he would stand by and watch their efforts a little disdainfully. Then he would begin to shout and encourage them, in the true square-rigged style. And every time they brought their weight down upon the rope, he would sing out a different phrase: "*Haul* away! *Now*, boys! *All* together! *Well*, then! *Heave* away! *Heave* 'n' raise the dead!" It really did encourage them, too. I used to feel that he would break into a chantey, next.

For two or three days I was mightily teased by the crew. They had discovered, much to my relief, that I wasn't seasick, and in all probability shouldn't be. So they had let up on that subject. But there was another possibility, which they noticed in a flash. It was the thought that I might be irritated if they accused me of being homesick. In vain I turned upon them. Even the mate, even the cook himself, shared the fun. If I were discovered looking down into the water, or up at the constantly swinging reef points; even if I sat on the saddle of the spanker boom and looked out over the sea, one of them would come along and tap me meaningly on the shoulder, saying: "Well, Barbara, gettin' homesick?" Once the cook made me almost furious. I was sitting on his galley doorstep, silent for a moment, and suddenly he launched this remark at me: "Ye're gettin' terrible homesick, ain't you?" I had discovered the futility of trying to prevent these taunts. I simply said: I never get homesick, and I'm not now." But when, after a little talk, I started to walk aft, the cook said: "You don't need t' go away mad!" "Mad?" said I. "What under the sun should I be mad about?" And then: "It's just a saying," said he.

It was the same if I expressed a desire for a little more wind, like what we had had before. Then I was accused of "wantin' to get there too quick." And even when, as we approached the entrance to the harbor a few days afterwards, I said something about how beautiful it was, they immediately asserted that I was eager "to be gettin' ashore." But I refused to be more than secretly irritated at the teasing of the crew I had so longed to sail with.

Roy had a harmonica. There was a great deal of merry-making in the fo'c'sle with it. Oftentimes the bo's'n, whose place is aft, and who is not supposed to join in with the crew too freely, would go into the fo'c'sle and ask Roy to play this tune or that. I used to ask Roy what were some of the things which he played — such things as "Oh, Katherina!" " 'Twas three o'-clock in the morning," and "The Rosewood Casket." He really managed his little harmonica very well, using a cup for a sounding-post. Sometimes Richardson played it; he was even more brilliant, but not so careful. Oftentimes Roy would play it out on deck, sitting on the covers of the hatchways; or he would play it from within the fo'c'sle.

Once when I was in the galley with the cook I heard music from the fo'c'sle, and on opening the little sliding door I beheld Roy, with his harmonica, playing a brisk waltz and waltzing gaily around the fo'c'sle to his own music[2] — all in a space about the size of an ordinary dining-table. He was turning round and round, taking tiny steps. This was one of the most amusing things I saw among the crew.

The Voyage of the Norman D.

He grinned rather sheepishly when he saw that I was watching him, and there followed quite a parley about dancing of one kind and another. This led to a gathering of the crew, and everyone got to talking about it. I happened, though somewhat in jest, to ask Bill if he could dance a sailor's hornpipe. But Bill rather sadly shook his head, and Bob struck in scornfully, and said: "Oh, him! He couldn't dance a cow's hornpipe."

"No," said Bill, "none o' the family are much good as dancers!"

"Dick's a good dancer."

"Yes, and a good waltzer, too."

The difference between a dancer and a waltzer I never did find out. But I have always wished that Bill *could* dance the sailor's hornpipe.

* * *

THE next day (the seventh out) the breeze was dying down. There was none of the whitecapped fierceness of the day before; nothing but a gentle, easy wash — a pretty good sailing breeze if only it had been from a different direction. But it was holding to northeast like grim death. It was a dull, sad day. Early, there was a curtain, a thick veil, of white sea fog over the coast, so that we couldn't see it and didn't know how near it was. This rather disturbed the old man, and he was afraid to pick up anchor. It was slightly warmer than the day before, because there was so much less wind. Later, the fog lifted, and we saw the long, low, very black and dismal shore line of Cape Sable, farther off than we had suspected, lying under the fog.

There were large islands about, and the captain was kept at work for some time with his charts, finding out exactly where we were. He finally discovered that we were in what is called Pubnico Harbor. I didn't feel that it was much of a harbor: we were exposed to the full force of nearly all weathers.

Dinner that day started out to be as awkward and uncomfortable as ever, what with the cook's hatred and the mate's and my embarrassment. The ship was still at anchor; indeed, the captain had definitely agreed with the mate that we should not get under way without the wind's changing. But the captain seemed to be blissfully unconscious of all the awkwardness, and he sat there smiling away and rattling on endlessly. He was just saying: "When I came back from Florida — " and then he suddenly decided that he should like a cigarette to go with his strong black tea. He left us abruptly to get one. While he was gone, the cook had an opportunity of which he was not slow to take advantage. He leaned 'way over toward us from his sentinel's post and said in a hoarse whisper: "Come back from Floridy, did he? Hm! It's a wonder the turkey buzzards didn't get him." He said this in such a deep, ominous voice that I felt myself almost shivering. What a piratical little old man!

That was not the last of it. The captain returned, and we fell to talking about wolves. I don't know what he knew about them, but he seemed to find plenty to say about anything at all, and a lot left over. The meal was shortly over, and again the cook bent down and whispered to us: "Hm! I guess the wolves wouldn't want *him* much — nothin' there but bones." Mutiny!

I'm sure that a mutiny would really have risen if we had had a crew of any spirit at all. I can readily imagine the cook standing up on top of a keg of rum, addressing the crew as ringleader, and I can imagine his carrying them with him — oh, how he would carry them! — and I can see them all drawing their cutlasses, flashing them aloft, and crying out: "All hail to the steward!" But it was a dull crew — a gloomy, sad, dejected, rather too good-natured crew, usually. Such things would not go with them. They were quite content to *talk* about the old man, to criticize him in every way that they could think of.

* * *

I HAD a good talk with the mate that afternoon — or, rather, a good listening to the mate. The bo's'n had been painting up the engine-room; he had painted the machinery red, black, and green. Very gay it looked, and he was rather proud of his work, and took me in to see it. I told him it was a fine job, and we had a minute of conversation, Bob telling me something about the machinery, with a sprinkling of talk concerning the old man. Then I went to see Bill, who was off duty at that moment. I asked him if he didn't think Bob had done a good job in the engine-room. And this was his reply:

"Oh, yes, pretty good for Bob. But it's nothin' compared to the job I done once, when I was bo's'n on a four-masted schooner. I allus did have a craze for neatness, everythin' in *order*. Well, that engine-room o' theirs was a *mess* when they enlisted me as bo's'n. I niver seen a worse mess. 'N' I went right to work, 'n' I scraped the floor, 'n' the walls, 'n' the ceiling, 'n' I painted all the wheels and the engine all over agin, 'n' I varnished the floor, 'n' I scrubbed it all up spick and span as could be. Well, the skipper knowed that I was forrard, workin' there, 'n' one day he come forrard to see about it. Well, I had that place so clean that you could go in there in a clean white shirt 'n' run the engine 'n' niver get a speck of dirt or grease on it. Well, the skipper was awful pleased, 'n' he said: 'Bo's'n, I'm proud o' that job — I niver had a engine-room lookin' so good as that.' Well, I was a young man then, and I was proud, I tell you!"

That day proved, except for the wonderful remarks of the cook, to be quite monotonous. If we had been sailing, with the mudhook lifted, it really wouldn't have made much difference, in that gloom and fog. The sea was very mysterious. The wild gale had vanished, but there was quite a swash left over. We stayed there all day, and rolled.

And we rolled in our bunks all night, to a jingling of bottles in the medicine-cabinet, the banging of doors, and the yelling of Bill as he strove to wake up Bob every four hours. The next day, waking up to find the schooner still rolling crazily about, we went out on deck, very curious to find out what the weather was doing. It gave us a cold, cold reception. The first thing I saw was the crazy motion of the deck, and next I saw the sea where the sky ought to be, and then the sky where the sea ought to be. The fog had gathered around us thickly and menacingly, saturating the air with brine, dismal and wet to breathe. It curled around us in weird and fantastic shapes, like mountain mist, but not so white and beautiful.

We could just see the bow of the vessel from where we were, aft, and we could clearly see that thick fog wafting across through the jibs, above the bowsprit. The schooner was in a mysterious little world of her own — a world of about a hundred feet on all sides; beyond it, blankness and silence. It was tangible space; you could see nothing — the nothingness — so clearly. The ghostly ocean had turned to a silver-gray, and it slipped away beneath us and fell back, then rose and rose again, slidingly, mingling with the sky. We could not distinguish between the swells even so much as when it was clear. I would be looking steadfastly at what used to be the sky: then, suddenly, I would see nothing but those shifting waters there, and then they would fall back, and down, and again there was a wheeling sky of fog.

The Voyage of the Norman D.

* * *

WHILE I was still down in the cabin, early that morning, a strange sound had startled me — a roaring drone, very sinister and terrible. At first, alarmed, I had wondered in vain what it was. But when I went on deck and saw that fog I knew immediately: the ship's foghorn. Do you know what I thought of when I first recognized it? I thought of Billy Bones, who used to blow through his nose "like a foghorn." I was curious to see how it was worked, but there wasn't time before breakfast. I went down with a hearty appetite, encouraged by that strong briny smell.

I don't know when I had been amused by the old captain so much as I was just after the meal, when, as we all started to go out on deck together, he began to explain. We went up the steep, small steps before him, but he followed us. He began down in the cabin to ejaculate: "Well, folks, this is a mull! A regular mull. It's a June mull! A regular June mull." And then, following us out on to the deck, he kept on in a low monotone: "Yes, folks, it certainly is a mull — a regular mull — a June mull — a regular June mull! We have these regular mulls every June. Yes, folks, it's just what I expected. A mull! That's what it is! A regular June mull!" (When I got home, after adventures yet to be reported, I immediately went to my dictionary to look up the word "mull." It seems to have all meanings except that of a spell of foggy weather. And I don't at all know what was meant, if not that. Possibly it was Captain Avery's own invention — that word; and possibly that was why he enjoyed saying it so much.

Captain Avery had about ten thousand calendars in that after cabin; calendars, apparently, from all parts of the world. They lined the walls of every bunk compartment. (Actually, I think there were about nineteen, or some odd number like that.) Of them all, there were a very few of 1927, from which they reached back as far as 1922. I went exploring among them, on the suggestion of my shipmate, to see in what months they left off. And, strange to relate, I found only three which got as far as December. A few left off in April, May, July; a large majority stopped short in various *Junes*.

"I believe the old man's been keeping count of June mulls!" said my shipmate.

"It certainly looks so," said I.

This was about the wettest day we had; certainly the wettest so far. The sheets were dripping, and when, later, we got under way we found them cold, stiff, and very hard to handle. As for the sails, it was quite impossible to sit under or near them: they kept shedding icy drops of concentrated sea fog down the back of one's neck.

Two or three times we went into the galley to get warm. Its stove was always roaring during this cold weather, and the door was kept shut, seemingly to keep the gravy smell in as well as the heat. Always our visits were made exciting by piratical remarks. Once I was sitting on the galley doorstep with my head out in the fog; my shipmate was farther back inside; and the cook was standing by the cupboards, making dough. The remark was not intended for my ears, but I overheard it. He had begun by saying, in all probability, profane things about Captain Avery, crowning his talk with this: " 'F you folks wasn't aboard, I'd be tempted to p'ison the food!"

I was so stunned by this that I couldn't believe I had heard aright, and I turned upon the steward, saying: "What was that, cook?" Then he felt abashed, I think; anyway, he said: "Hm! I guess it's as well you didn't hear."

* * *

THE old man sat still at anchor for a great part of the day. Then he had an idea the wind was shifting slightly to the south. Really it was just a little whim of the breeze, but the old man was evidently eager to arrive at Bridgewater, and, without any *yoho*-ing from that gloomy crew, the engine was started, and the mudhook came up through the intense fog, looking more than ever like a ghostly skeleton.

Shortly after that the mate and I had a marvellous talk behind the fo'c'sle, sitting side by side on the roof of it. The mate began by saying what a blankety-blank fool he thought the old man was:

"Here we was, sitting comfortable at anchor, knowin' where we was, in Pubnico Harbor. Now here the breeze swings off a quarter point to sou'. Well, the old man takes that too serious, specially when there ain't no wind nohow. So up with the mudhook, and up with the sails into the fog, and off we starts. *Now* look at us! There are the sails flappin' and flappin', and here is we rollin' and beatin' around. The fool! He'll lose his reck'nin', sure. I know he will! Well, if *I* had anything to say about it, I wouldn't 'a' tried it!

"Well, Barbara, how you feeling now?"

"Oh, I'm first-rate, mate!"

"Well, you've done fine. I thought sure you'd be sick."

"Yes, and you acted kind of as though it would have been a grand joke if I had been, too."

"Oh, but I was just teasin' you. I niver had a young sister to play with, and now one comes along quite handy, and I can't help it."

"Yes, you were teasing, all right! But as for the cook, I think he'd have been awfully glad if I had been moderately sick."

"The steward? Sure, he'd 'a' been glad enough to see you sick. But as for me, I hoped you wouldn't be — 'cos, I'll tell it to you before your face or behind your back, you're the smartest li'l girl I ever seen aboard of a vessel yit. Ye're not afraid t' ask questions, an' ye're not afraid t' work, neither."

"Well, mate, I've always wanted to go sailing, and now that I'm doing it I might as well chip in and help, and learn."

"Sure! Well, not everyone would."

And then, after that gallant remark, the mate fell to telling me about the state of affairs at home.

"You know, Barbara, when I got married, I was married on a Monday, and I went off t' sea agin Tuesday. I didn't come back home fer six months. 'N' then I stayed home all day Monday, 'n' went off t' sea agin Tuesday. Well, it did seem kind of tough at the time, but now I'm glad I don't see m' wife very often. Y' see, it keeps us from gettin' tired of each other. Now, when I go home, we have more fun! We're just like a couple o' kids. We sit together and bicker and bicker all th' time.

"Well, my wife does a great deal in the line of fancy 'mbroidery. She can do all kinds of work of that kind, and she does love to do it. So she sits at one end of the table, evenings, with some work of that kind, and I sit at the other end, whittlin' or carving with wood, and we do have a good time."

"Do you do much whittling and wood-carving, mate?"

"Yes, I do quite a bit. And I have a lot of fun doing it, too. I like nothin' better than to take a block of good wood, and a good knife (only I never have one), and sit by the fire in the stove, to carve something. I did a full-rigged ship model once — oh! I wish you could 'a' seen her, Barbara; she was a beauty! It took me about two weeks around Christmas-time to make her. Well, a friend of mine, a sea captain, came t' see me, 'n' he asked if he could have her. 'What'll you give for her?' I says. 'Well, shipmate, what do you ask?' 'Oh, you can have her fer five dollars,' I says. So he give me five dollars fer her. Then, later, he told me that he had been offered sixty dollars for that ship of mine, 'n' that he had refused to sell her fer that!

"Yes, I seem to be gifted in that line. I did a violin once, from a model of an old one that a friend o' mine had. I worked on it all summer, 'n' another friend played on it fer a long time. I had a lot of fun making it. But the hardest part was making the holes fer the pegs. Y' see, they are so much narrower on the inside than on the outside that it's very hard to get at them. Well, I strung her up, 'n' she made a good little violin.

" 'N' I do quite a little in the painting line, too. I used t' do water-color sketches of full-rigged ships, with the sky 'n' the sea all painted in, and painted good, too. I used t' sell 'em fer a dollar apiece. Yes, I had considerable thought of bein' an artist. But there wasn't enough money, 'n' I had t' get out and earn, so I went t' sea. 'N' at sea I stayed, 'n' I guess I always will. Y' see, I can carve, and I can paint, but here I am wasting my life with Cap'n Avery — sixty per month. It seems hard. I think I'll resign at Bridgewater. But, ye see, I don't want t' do the old man any harm. I wouldn't harm him fer worlds; not me. 'N' if I did resign, then the hull crew would. Didn't ye hear what Richardson said about me holdin' the crew together? Well, that's a fact."

"How many are there in your family?"

"Well, there was twenty births in the family, but there are only eight now. Some o' them died in the war, some o' them died of sickness. I have one little brother that I haven't seen since he was five months old. An' when Mother died, there I was, th' oldest of the family, with a little sister ten years old, and another one only eight — an' I tell you, I felt powerful lonely. Well, I went right off to sea, and left the young children with an aunt. Now they's almost all married, and has children of their own. As fer myself, I have three children — two sons and a daughter."

He picked up a little sliver from a board which was left over from the lumber cargo, opened his knife, and carved away at it.

(It is funny about Bill's knives. He told me he had about four around on the schooner somewhere, and that they kept cropping up here and there and then disappearing, and that Bob had two or three of them. Almost every one is broken. It seems that Bill isn't wealthy enough to buy real knives, so he buys a thousand cheap tin affairs which last about five minutes. I told him, partly in joke, that I should certainly buy him a jackknife the first thing when I got back to New Haven, and send it up to Bridgewater before the schooner sailed.) He carved that sliver, with amazing speed, into a delightful little rowboat with a very accurate keel and lovely lines along the gunwales. He tossed it over to me immediately. I have that little boat now — just about my only tangible remembrance of Mate Bill and the *Norman D.*

It was Bill's watch above, but he didn't seem to have anything in particular to do, and he was evidently glad to have someone to talk to. The silence and gloom, with blasts from the foghorn every now and then, struck home upon everyone's senses. I began to ask Bill the names of various things aboard. I learned, on that day, a lot of ropes and blocks; he answered every question carefully and clearly. He was probably glad to air his knowledge a little.

"By the way, mate," said I, "I thought that when the booms and sails are to starboard, then you're on the port tack, and that when the booms and sails are to port, then you're on the starboard tack. Is that so?"

"Yes, that's right."

"Well, when I asked the cook this morning about the foghorn, he said that there is one blast when you're on the port tack, two when you're on the starboard tack, and three when you're running. We're on the port tack now, according to you, but they are giving the horn two blasts."

"No, the steward's got you all twisted round. It's one on the starboard tack, two on the port, and three running."

"Well, I wondered who was wrong."

"Now, I don't like that at all," said Bill. "That's just like the steward, to fool you that way. Now, I like to answer questions that are asked me, as well as I know how. But him! No, you can never tell with him. And, you see, he makes you disbelieve me, and then I get in wrong there."

"No, I didn't disbelieve you, mate. I thought that, ten to one, the cook was wrong."

"Yes, he's wrong. That is, I was always learned the way I told you. That may not be right, but it's the way I was learned."

So we sat there in that ghostly fog, and discussed multitudinous little subjects — about sailing vessels, mostly — and I began to think that I had never known anyone more entertaining than Mate Bill. He was my idea of a real sailor.

When we dropped anchor during that wild night, it had evidently been over a clayey bottom; the anchor had three or four good-sized lumps of sticky gray clay on it. I fell to scraping it off, and Bill scraped some off, too. I started molding it in my hands until I had got it to the right texture; then I showed Bill how I had been taught to make pottery out of it, first making a smooth round of clay for the bottom, then rolling out long slender coils of it, and coiling it on to that bottom round, coil after coil, and in that way building up a jar or bowl. I loved that clay, because it was full of little shells and pebbles which had become stuck into it; I found some delightful ones. Then I started making two blocks, absolutely smooth, and with sharp corners. I put them down on the bulwarks beside the cathead to dry. It was a secret between Bill and me that they were to heave at the old man, when they dried and became hard, if he came forward interfering in what was none of his business.

***

BILL and I must have been talking and playing there on the fo'c'sle well over an hour, when suddenly there came a whoop from aft. Immediately everyone was excited. It was that infernal "Here, boys! Here, boys! Here, boys!" Since it was the mate's watch, or supposed to be, and since it was probably growing upon Bill's conscience that he had been idling for longer than he should have, he left me with a bound, crossed the rolling deck in three more leaps, and was beside the skipper. As for me, I was eager to find out what the disturbance was, and I started to climb down from the roof of the fo'c'sle to see for myself. But I was unable to cross the deck with the speed and agility of the mate; I walked slowly, though steadily, and climbed with some difficulty up the poop deck stairs. I beheld a very amazing sight. The captain had a boat hook down over the port side of the schooner, with something hooked on to the end of it — a crate or box of some kind, as it looked. Evidently, when he had once got it hooked, it had been too heavy for him, and he had been unable to hold it, but, unwilling to let go, on the chance that it might be something worth having, he had started whooping for help. Now the whole crew had gathered there, and they all had boat hooks down, and were hauling it up. It was a large, heavy, mysterious box, and it rattled meaningly from within. *What* could it be? Was it gold? Mightn't it be treasure? Supposing it were! Oh, how marvellously piratical! My imagination reigned supreme over my common sense then.

But things were becoming confused now. There were so many of the crew there, and so many boat hooks all struggling for a grasp on that one box, that everyone was getting in everyone else's way, and the captain, as was his custom, was becoming terribly excited. The red spot was glowing on his cheek, and his eyes were flustered and wild. The mate was trying desperately to shove him out of the way, but he held on to his boat hook stubbornly, and held the boat hook around the rope with which the thing was tied, and, in resistance to the mate, he was yelling out in a horrible voice: "Let go! Let go! Let go! Let me go! Let go!" — followed by a furious cascade of oaths. But the mate gently ushered the old man out of the way, where he sank back upon the deckhouse, exhausted, still grasping the boat hook.

That helped a lot; there was much less confusion. And, although the captain still gurgled out delicious oaths now and then, the crew kept their heads pretty well, and brought the great box slowly over the taffrail. What was within? I could hardly contain myself. By the wicked glint in the old man's eyes — a glint like that of an eagle's or a hawk's — I knew that he had some avaricious hopes that it was a box of gold.

The crew slid off the rope, and opened the crate. Was it gold? What was it? Everyone peered over everyone else's shoulders. *Was* it gold — gleaming gold? It was —

It was —

I can hardly bear to say. Not that it was disappointing to me particularly, because my sense had begun to come back and take revenge on my piratical imagination. Of course, thought I, in this modern time it couldn't be gold; if this had happened in the days of Blackbeard or John Flint, it might have been. Besides, a box of gold would sink, not float serenely past. It was — No shrinking, now; I have got to tell. One more effort!

It was — a box of clams! hundreds and hundreds of clams. At first we thought that they were good, and this rather tickled the cook, who, as usual when anything was going on, had come out of the galley, his apron strings flopping behind him. But after they had broken open five or six and tasted them —

The old man had pretty well recovered by this time, and in

exasperated tones he ordered the bo's'n to heave the box overboard. But they had already dumped about half of the clams out upon the deck in sorting them over, and there was an oily mess there. The bo's'n picked up the box, staggered under it, and almost had it over the taffrail, when the weight overwhelmed him, and again he staggered backwards under it, spilling out most of the clams. A mighty oath followed from the enraged bo's'n; then he shouted out to the mate: "Here, give a hand with the cursed thing!" Together they got it over; whereupon the bo's'n fetched a shovel and scooped the rest of the mess over.

That was done, and it certainly did leave the crew in a sullen, mutinous condition. "The idea," they cursed "— to put us to that trouble over an old box of rotten clams!" The skipper, his greediness disappointed, was shamefacedly pacing the deck, while the cook retired into the galley, muttering: "Oh, Lordy! Lordy!"

* * *

THE sea still heaved and pulsated strangely, rose and slid back into its own deep hollows. All day the fog scudded across, with its briny smell. It seemed to be clutching you in its cold, wet arms, and it saturated you. All you could breathe was that damp, salt wetness. There were times when we could barely see the tip of the flying jibboom from aft, and there were other times when the sun tried its best to shine through, and we could see up there the feeble yellow splotch of it. And it was bitter cold — a wet, miserable cold, not the fresh cold of the former breeze.

There is nothing more uncanny than passing a bell buoy or a whistling buoy in such weather. All sense of direction is lost. To tell which way we were heading, or from which way the wind was coming, I saw even the crew go up aft to look at the compass. Everything was a moving space, swirling slowly around and around us. Approaching a buoy, you hear first a loud whistling and droning somewhere far off in the future; and, because you can't see it, it makes you shudder. Sometimes you think it's to starboard, and sometimes you are sure it's to port, and then you have the strangest feeling that it's dead astern. But how can it be astern, you ask yourself, when you haven't yet passed it? You can't definitely tell where it is until you come within sight of it, or unless you have sea ears trained for such things. You become haunted with the strange music of that whistler, and you listen and listen for it, to find out *where* it is. But it mocks you, and dodges you, and plays hide and seek with you, knowing itself quite safe beneath the curtain of fog.

Yes, you feel that it is a mournful and mocking sound, that calling. And then, perhaps the fog breaks for an instant, and you see the thing which has been playing with you. You see it looming vaguely, strangely, from sea and fog all mixed together — a great red monster lifting up its head to howl, a haunted brick-red castle, rocking there amid the swell. And then it roars or tolls its bell again, and you feel that it has lifted its voice in despair at being discovered.

Watching a buoy, we could see very clearly how slowly the ship was making headway, and how fast she was making leeway. We felt, seeing a thing like that looming at us from the depths of the sea, more alone and queer, more desolate than ever. Again that sense of solitude overwhelmed us.

This happened once or twice that day. But the captain had lost his reckoning — absolutely lost it! His instruments depended upon the sun, and there was none of that. Dead reckoning was of no use, because of the leeway, and the no wind, and the swell. When we passed a buoy which the captain didn't understand, he and the mate got together on the cabin floor, on their knees and elbows, over the chart, one on each side of it, to work out the position.

Neither could come to a definite solution of that buoy, and the captain appeared nervous and worried. He would come on deck, saying: "If there's anything I hate, it's these June mulls!" And then the mate would say, very confidentially, to me: "It's his own fault, the withered old fool. If he'd done what he oughter have done, stayed right there where he knew where he was, we wouldn't have got into this trouble. Sometimes I think the old fellow's got no more sense than a baby."

There was nothing much to be done; at least, if there were anything the captain certainly showed his ignorance of it. Some of the crew thought that he ought to drop anchor now, before they got into a hole somewhere alongshore. But the old man kept a-going, and we beat about, blowing that infernal horn, all day. What with the gloom, the silence, the fog, the wetness and coldness, and that horn at regular intervals, we were pretty tired by evening, and ready enough to drop into our bunks. I had tried pumping the horn a little, and found that I enjoyed the sound somewhat more when I helped to make it.

There is one amusing detail connected with that horn which I mustn't forget. It was a rather rickety old affair, and if you pumped it too furiously it would stop its long, steady drone and go off into croaking falsetto whoops. It was a commonly agreed fact among the crew that, when it did this, it was exactly like the old man's voice. When the old man pumped his voice too hard, it, too, would go off into the same sort of croaking whoops. And the crew — especially, of course, Bob, who, when it was his trick at the horn, always, after pumping it correctly for a few seconds, let it go off into those whoops — thought it a great joke to make the horn echo the old man's excitement. It all disgusted the old cook very much. He would sit in the galley door, with a roaring fire in the galley stove (to which we would come in at frequent intervals for a warming-up), muttering his favorite mutter of "Oh, Lordy! Lordy!" and saying that it was all nonsense, that business. But it seemed rather to tickle the mate, who, with his customary malicious chuckles, would pretend to be rather disgusted, but whose eyes would twinkle in that piratical way which made me think that he really enjoyed the joke.

* * *

WE beat about, hard-aleeing, all the afternoon. That awful "Hard alee!" whoop of the skipper sounded inexpressibly dismal, echoing through the fog, and echoed by the foghorn. After a diverting yarn from the steward, which I shall soon repeat, we slept in the midst of the roll, and were grateful for the privilege.

The cook, returning after supper from the cabin with his basket of food and dirty dishes, saw the two of us promenading the decks in the fog, apparently doing just about nothing, and he decided that it was a bully good chance for talking. He stood there securely, holding his basket, and rattled on and on and on until I felt pretty sure there would be no finish, ever. I missed, unfortunately, the beginning of the tale; not realizing what we were in for, I had started walking forward, looking over the bulwarks. When I returned, the yarn was *in medias res*. The cook, it seemed, was in a three-masted schooner which was going to race a four-masted schooner from somewhere to somewhere else, to find out which was the better vessel. As I missed the beginning, I don't know any more about it. The cook was just saying, with the most dramatic gesticulation I had ever seen:

" — Well, it was a fine day, that day we was goin' to race; good sailin' breeze, everythin' just dandy. But luck seemed to be agin us. We manned the capstan at the same time as the crew of t' other vessel, an' we was workin' away good and brisk, but it didn't seem t' work right. Well, we had t' stop heavin' and see what was the matter. It took a good long time t' get it fixed, 'n' then 'twarn't fixed right, so we had a bully hard time gettin' the anchor up. By this time, the four-master was out o' the harbor, gettin' a good breeze, 'n' a'most out o' sight. Then we started t' get our centerboard down. But that didn't work right, neither, and try as we might, we couldn't get her down. We got grease 'n' poured it down, and I brought soap from the galley, 'n' we worked away 'n' worked away at it. Well, finally we got her down, 'n' then we got our sails up 'n' were off.

"I thought we was niver goin' out o' that harbor. There wasn't much wind there, 'n' we went so *slow!* Well, we got a good breeze after a time, 'n' then we did tear along. But the *Edward Coles* was 'way out o' sight, 'n' we was pretty sure we was niver goin' to catch up with her. The next mornin' there was quite a argyment in the after cabin as t' where she was. Some held she was t' windward of us, some held to leeward, and some says she was straight astern. The cap'n said she was t' windward. But I knowed better. Says I: 'No, sir, she ain't t' windward, she's astern of us.' 'Oh, Si, it's impossible. I know she's t' windward.' 'I'll wager with you she's astern,' says I. 'I won't wager with you, Si, 'cause you'll on'y lose yer money. She's t' windward.' 'What do you think, mate?' says I t' the chief mate. 'Oh, I think she's t' windward.' 'Sir,' says I, 'I 'nsist I'll wager with you. Now I'll put up ten dollars agin your ten cents, 'n' we'll see 'bout it.' 'No, Si,' says he, 'I won't make a wager like that.' 'Oh, sir,' says I, 'y' ain't got no sportin' blood in you. Come on, now, wager ten cents agnst my ten dollars! We'll see who's right this time!'

" 'Now, Si,' says he, 'y' must know where th' schooner is, t' make a wager like that. Otherwise ye'd niver put up ten dollars aginst ten cents.' 'Oh, go on, sir, wager with me!' says I. 'Well, Si, but you must know something t' make a wager like that.' Well, I coaxed, 'n' I coaxed, 'n' I coaxed, but fer the life of me I couldn't make him put up ten cents. Then says I: 'Sir, y' ain't got no sportin' blood in you, 'n' I'm goin' t' tell you what I know. You go up halfway in th' mizzen riggin', 'n' you'll see the *Edward Coles* astern of us.' Well, the skipper banged his fist down on th' cabin table, 'n' jumped up 'n' ran on deck. He went right up halfway into the mizzen rigging, 'n' then he slapped his leg 'n' hollers out: 'By Godfrey almighty, there's the *Edward Coles*! You're right, Si, there she be.' How'd I know? Well, o' course I'd a been up in the mizzen riggin' early that mornin', 'n' I seen her astern of us.

"Well, we won that race by a good long shot, I'll say, now!"

And then I saw the apron strings dangling, as the old man walked sedately back into the galley with his basket of dishes, leaving us alone in the cold, wet fog.

THE fog swept about the little ship all night. The first thing I saw when I thrust myself out of the cabin was Richardson, at the helm. He was bunched up in a massive overcoat, and his shoulders were shrugged up the way they always were in cold weather. He was dripping wet, and standing in the center of a cloud of fog, which swept around him menacingly, like the white, floating shroud of a ghost. However, it was not so thick, and the sun made on it a kind of shimmering rainbow, which the crew called a "fog eater." It was very mysterious and lovely to see that path of faint iridescence, glimmering in a ghostly way through the monotonous whiteness. There was no more wind than the day before, perhaps not even so much, and I think there was more of a roll than I had known on any of the previous days. I had a great deal of fun practising walking about on the decks. If there had been much more of a roll, the crew said, she would have been rolling water on her decks. As it was, I saw none of that.

Of course the sails, the booms, the rigging, the tackle were all making their infernal racket — a racket which wears on your sense even more than the silence of the fog. Here the mate gave me a very quaint descriptive sentence. Said he: "I hate to sit here and listen to her flap her wings and shake her feathers." How like flapping wings and shaking feathers it sounded!

We went in pretty close to some land or other, but as the captain had not yet got his bearings, we didn't know what it was. We had an idea that we were somewhere near the mouth of the Lahave River, where we wanted to go. There was nothing much to be done except drive on until the weather cleared off. The captain said that there was no earthly use in trying to keep a-going without any wind. "We've got t' have a breeze t' sail, 'n' that's all there is to it." So he decided to drop anchor, before we should be carried ashore by our leeway. "Get down the outer jib, boys!" he bellowed out, "flyin' jib, 'n' jib!" Then the mate, on the fo'c'sle deck: "Get down the outer jib, sir!" Then the bo's'n, from the jib halyards: "Get down the outer jib, sir!" in his usual mocking voice. But then, just as they were about to get down the forestaysail also, the captain's voice rang out again: "Hold on the forestaysail a minute!" And the mate: "Hold on the forestaysail a minute, sir!" And the bo's'n: "Hold on the forestaysail a minute, sir!" The captain had noticed a tiny breath of air rising, and now he commanded the jibs to be hauled up again. Once more we set sail — or set jibs, rather — and started off. We were going a little bit faster, but still the schooner was flapping her wings and shaking her feathers.

The Voyage of the Norman D.

I went forrard to have a small talk with the mate. "Quite a little trouble to no purpose, wasn't it?" said I.

"Well, 's long's it pleases him, all right," replied Mate Bill.

"Well, mate, are we still off Cape Sable?" (This was a great joke among the crew, because of waking up so many mornings in succession to be told that we were off Cape Sable.)

"Hanged if *I* know where we are! The old man doesn't know, neither, 'n' we can't find out 'ntil this pesky fog clears away. But I wish th' skipper would get some sense in 's head 'n' let us stay at anchor, afore we gets into any worse scrape 'n this. We'll be aground, next."

Indeed, the old man did appear to be extremely nervous. "If there's anything I hate, it's these June mulls!" he would say, over and over. He always appeared to be shivering and shaking, and he had acquired a terrific cold in his head. When he came down for meals, I noticed that he could barely eat and drink, his hands were quivering and shaking so. Yes, the old man was certainly alarmed over something — over losing his bearings, and being shut in by fog. But he didn't anchor. While there was a breath of air stirring, he kept the schooner to her course, and we went sailing very, very slowly up the coast of Nova Scotia.

About the only happening that afternoon that was in the least piratical occurred when I went forward to have a chin with the crew, and found no one there. The galley and the fo'c'sle were both quite deserted. The captain strode by once as I was talking to Bob at the wheel, and said: "Don't talk to the helmsman, Barbara — it distracts him." So I hadn't talked again with anyone at the wheel. Yes, the helmsman was at his trick, the lookout was at the foghorn, and — there was no one else in evidence. How strange! I went exploring. I happened to look into the engine-room — and, lo! there they all were. The cook was there, leaning against the wall with one elbow, the other hand on his hip, his legs crossed, looking very important. The mate was there, and his dark, piratical eyes were full of the light of mutiny. The bo's'n was there, with his customary careless, fresh look. Irish Bill was there, and his rather wicked Irish eyes were gleaming. *What were they doing?* I asked myself.

"What's going on?" said I. "You look as mischievous as though you were concocting a mutiny. *Are* you?"

"Oh, we're justy talkin'," explained Bill.

" 'N' plannin' some deviltry," said the cook.

"I see," said I.

I really had an idea that they weren't so innocent as they pretended. They probably wouldn't have let me into their secrets anyhow. But I knew the man to go to — a special friend of the cook's, to whom the cook confided everything in fullest detail: my shipmate.

From him I discovered startling things. I didn't inquire too closely, but I imagine they came from the cook. It seems that the crew had gathered in the engine-room for the purpose of a conference on writing *a letter of complaint against Captain Avery.* They were agreeing to stand by each other in this mutiny like brothers — *and to sign their names to this letter!* I'd wager all the pirate treasure ever buried that it was the cook who suggested it.

"I guess the cook would sign *his* name, all right!" said I.

"Oh, he'd sign his name all over the letter," said my shipmate.

That set me thinking, I tell you. I really wished that the cook or Mate Bill would confide in me enough to tell me the story. But evidently they would go up to a certain point with me, such as jesting about the old man, but not far enough to reveal to me such deep and dangerous secrets. They didn't need to worry: for the world I wouldn't have betrayed them!

* * *

The Voyage of the Norman D.

AS usual, we turned in early. That night I was so unfortunate as to sleep soundly through a happening which I was very sorry to miss. Perhaps it was owing to the fact that Mate Bill had been having a long conference with the two of us that night. We had been sitting on the after hatchway, all in a row, and Mate Bill was showing us how to tie different knots. I really believe there isn't a knot in the world that he couldn't tie. He went on and on, showing us more and more complicated ones, even splicing. Every now and then he would say assuringly: "There! now you'll know how to tie that when you go home." But I confess that I was so dazzled with the multitude of twists and turns that I couldn't remember any of them until, later, I looked them all up in my dictionary. Perhaps it was with all these knots dancing in my head that I went to sleep so early and slept so soundly. Or perhaps it was because my hard, uncomfortable bunk was very snug and warm compared with the sea and the fog.

Or perhaps it was the delight of a certain thing which happened just before we turned in. It was this way: At first, during this knot-tying lesson, Mate Bill and I had been sitting there alone, but presently my shipmate emerged from the cabin doorway and joined us. Then the bo's'n, too, came strolling along from the direction of the fo'c'sle and began to contend against Mate Bill, wagering that Bill couldn't tie this knot or that, and Bill wagering that he could. Bob was very clever, too. Bill's challenging assertion that he couldn't braid nine strands he answered by promptly selecting the nine from a pile of old frayed rope, tying them to a backstay, and braiding them up. We had quite a little joke about the common square knot. After Bill had asked me many times if I could tie this, or if I could tie that, I replied by saying that the only good knot I could tie was the square knot. But Bob spoke up sneeringly and said that I couldn't tie a square knot. I said that I could, and was just about to select a strand and tie it, when Bill interposed and said: "Oh! I know what you mean, Bob. Your square knot ain't no good. 'Tain't a reg'lar square knot."

"Bet you can't tie it," said Bob.

"Well, what good is it when you have it tied?"

Bob now went to work and invented a very pretty, but useless, knot which, as Bill said, was the start for a square braid. But, after all, I was really right, and I had Bill to back me, and I selected my strand and tied my square knot. Bill took it and examined it very carefully; then he said that it was all right, and passed it on to Bob. Bob, too, looked at it, said in his turn that it was all right, and tossed it back to me. I doubt if there was ever such a fuss over a simple square knot.

As I said before, my shipmate had now come out from the warm depths of the cabin; and he was watching all this, standing over us on the poop deck. Now he called me, saying: "Come up here a minute, and see what you see!" And he went down and took my place beside Mate Bill. I looked down at the two of them; and truly it was a marvellous sight. It had now grown almost pitch dark, and I could just see the silhouettes of two forms, sitting there, their heads together, very still — still except for Mate Bill's fingers, which were busily at work in the tangles of some new knot. Behind them was the pile of old rope, like sacks of spoil in a heap — and they looked, those hunched figures, like two whispering spooks, sitting out there in the rain, "plannin' deviltry," as the cook would have said, and counting over their coins.

And I mustn't forget a rather piratical incident which happened just before we turned in. We had gone below, and were sitting together, talking about June mulls, when suddenly Mate Bill came down and went in to his bunk. It had started raining, and it was very dark. He had come down, in his wet-weather costume, to get a lantern. I didn't see him when he came down, but as soon as he had gone in to his bunk my shipmate nudged my arm and said in a whisper: "Watch the mate, now, when he comes out with the lantern. See if he doesn't look piratical!" I kept an eye on the small room of the mate, and presently we saw him come out, in his oilskins, sou'wester, and sea boots, all dripping wet, and lighted uncannily by the light of the lantern. Piratical! Never, in all the time before, had I seen him look so much so. He nodded good-night and clomped up the steps again, in his heavy boots.

Perhaps, as I said, all this had made my mind swirl with tangles of ropes and imaginings of pirates. Whatever the cause, I slept through the worst racket of the whole trip. The rest is hearsay — what I was told the next morning by the crew and my shipmate, who were amazed that I hadn't waked up.

The mate had told me on several occasions that in the month of June we were likely to have "squalls." At first I had got the idea that squalls were simply the cat's-paws which we see on inland lakes, only more violent. Later I decided, from what Bill said, that it only meant wind coming in spurts and then dying down. But at last I understood that squalls were raging thunderstorms which pass over the sea quickly, quickly, and are gone. Bill told me of several times, during his sailor career, when they had seen squalls coming from far off, sweeping wildly across the sea, blackening the sky, and had barely time to take the sails down before they were swamped in it. Squalls were very dangerous, the mate said, and whenever they were at all violent the sails would have to come down.

Well, we had one in the middle of that night. There were thunder, lightning, rain by the bucketful, and much stronger wind than any we had had. They described how the whole crew — even the cook, roused up out of his bunk — had scurried back and forth right over my head, to get down the sails at full speed. They wondered how on earth I could possibly have slept through that, let alone the howling of the wind, the rolling of the thunder, the brilliance of the lightning, and the tossing and plunging of the schooner. They crowned it by describing how the spanker gaff had been let down, one man at the peak halyards, the other at the throat halyards, and how the gaff had been let go in the tumult and come rattling down with a terrific crash on the deck house right over me. The old man, at this little mishap, had jumped with terror, and shrieked out a curse in so loud a voice that they wondered why that alone hadn't waked me.

The cook, of course, had his little word on this episode. He took me aside to the galley and told me in scornful terms how the old man had got excited and hectic, after his custom, and what a ridiculous crew we had, who didn't know how to do anything right, and did nothing but rush frantically around from here to there and back again, and how such foolishness wouldn't have been allowed in *his* day, when sailors were sailors, not landlubbers! Also, I was told how Bob, who, during all this, had been at the foghorn, had seen a good-sized steamer near by, and, very much afraid of running into her, had blown the foghorn so long, loud, and furiously that at length Mate Bill had to go forward and stop him. We had evidently been on the starboard tack, because Bob had intended to blow the horn once; but he had made it one such prodigiously long blast (the Mate said he must have blown it for a full ten minutes) that Bill was afraid the steamer wouldn't understand what on earth we *were* trying to do.

* * *

WHEN I first went on deck the next morning, I had a suspicion that all this might be a joke, or, at least, greatly exaggerated. But when I saw how every last wisp of the fog had blown away, leaving the air crystal clear, though still almost calm, I knew that it must have taken some violence to banish it all so quickly and completely. What a heavenly blue the sky was! It was one of those deep, quivering blues which I have so often seen at Sunapee. The sails shone sparklingly white, instead of their usual gray; the trucks of the masts were shining and clear-cut against that sky. We were quite near the shore, sailing before a steady breeze — just enough to keep the sails rounded, and to make the schooner yield and cant a little, yet not enough to make more than a delicate dash of foam along our sides.

During the whole trip I had not seen a lovelier shore. Even the shore of New Haven as we had left it on that memorable first day, with West Rock jutting up strangely; and the long green line of Martha's Vineyard as we had passed it; and the coast line of Rhode Island, on the afternoon of the first day — none of these was nearly so lovely as what now confronted us. It was a shore of low green hills, brighter than emerald in the sunlight and against the sky. They were high hills, yet with so gradual a slope that they presented an aspect of luxuriance and verdure, like a very mossy forest. Somber shadows were constantly passing over them like dark ghosts, reminding me of how the valleys had looked down at the foot of Moosilauke, with the shadows of slowly moving clouds on the radiance of the autumn trees. My first real glimpse of Nova Scotia! A beautiful land.

But the captain was no better off as to his bearings. He was sailing on with a rather doubtful air, looking again and again at his charts. It was the cook's opinion that he had passed Lahave River and was now on his way up to Lunenberg; but he added: " 'Tain't up t' me t' say anything." All of us were much relieved to find the fog cleared away, and everyone was much happier. Richardson, however, incurred two gibes that day from the mate. He had been set to work scrubbing off the deckhouse, while Mate Bill and I sat together discussing knots and watching him. Richardson, as was his custom, was doing the job very feebly and slowly, as though bored to death with it. At last the mate raised his head and said, with that wicked twinkle in his black eyes that I have described so many times: "Oh, hurry up, Dick, do! You're slower 'n an old woman with her washin'." Later in the day almost the same thing happened, when Richardson was scrubbing the highest part of the starboard fo'c'sle wall. "Don't be all day over it, Dick," said the mate. "Put some elbow-grease into it!" Whereat Richardson smiled feebly and tried to scrub a trifle harder.

As for me, the forbidden rigging looked more and more enticing now that the sails gleamed so white, and I was determined to have a climb. I had, to be sure, climbed about a little on one of the foggy days, when it had broken for a moment on our port bow, revealing a dark mass of land. The mate had gone up into the rigging to see if he could identify anything, and I had gone with him. But, though it was impressive to have seen the land lying over there like a mass of black fog, it wasn't really fun, and I had longed for a good day. Now, accordingly, I went aft and asked Captain Avery if I might run up to the crosstrees. "Oh, sure," he replied, "go ahead up, 'n' hold hard." So I started for the port mizzen rigging. But that was our leeward side, and the captain called me: "Don't go up on that side, Barbara. Allus go on the wind'ard."

"Why, Captain?"

"Well, y' see, when the schooner" (he always pronounced this *shownar*) "is heelin' over to loo'ard, the loo'ard riggin' gets slack, 'n' the wind'ard riggin' is taut all the while. 'N' then, too, the loo'ard riggin' 's much straighter, 'n' harder t' climb. That don't make no partic'lar difference to a sailor, 'coz 'f anything lets go, he kin always stop hisself, but with a greenhorn 't's different."

It was quite insulting to the pride of my sailor career to be called a greenhorn, but then, it was all right with me whatever they called me. I went to the starboard mizzen rigging, and up I climbed, with the same delightful sensations which I always had. But today there were other sensations, too. The schooner was rolling quite a little, and I had now, in the rigging, the same curious feelings that I had had running about the deck in our big gale. First the rigging seemed to slide away beneath my feet, and then it would be there before me. All the time I held very "hard" with my hands and went up steadily, though somewhat more slowly than usual. The mate called out to me to hold the shrouds, not the ratlines: because then, if a ratline happened to let go, I should still have something to hold to. I followed this advice, and very carefully kept one hand upon the rigging while I was low down, and both when I was high enough so that the ratlines were comfortably short and the shrouds near enough together. Still, the sway was very puzzling, and it increased as I mounted. I stuck to it, and when finally I sat down, rather breathless, on the crosstrees, I felt more as if I were on a seesaw than I have ever felt, even on a real seesaw. The crosstrees made graceful swoops and slow half circles through the air, and I saw the sea beneath me, first on one side, then on the other. It was very beautiful, but very alarming, too; and I felt more than ever like a sailor. That breath-taking instant when one gets from the crosstrees on to the ratlines and hangs for a moment over the sea was more breath-taking than ever. I thought of this, one of the sailor chanteys in *Iron Men and Wooden Ships*:

> When the foaming waves run mountains high,
> And the landsmen cry, 'All's gone,' sir,

The sailor hangs 'twixt sea and sky,
And he jokes with Davy Jones, sir!

For that instant I certainly felt the danger of joking with Davy. But the moment of peril was passed without mishap, and, after looking again at those beautiful hills, of which from up here I could see much more, I came down.

* * *

NOW a speck was descried by the hawk's eyes of the old man, on the starboard horizon (or, as he always pronounced it, *orison* with an *h* in front). Nearer and nearer it came, and finally it turned out to be just what I had hoped: a sail. Eagerly we watched, and as it skimmed slowly down along the skyline toward us we saw that it was another lofty four-masted schooner. But how insignificant it was away off there, how like a child's toy ship! We could see her masts, like matches, and her tiny gaffs and booms. The jibs were no more than slivers of silver thread, pointing away into the sky like fingers of moonlight; the topsails were four little snow-capped peaks along the edge of the sky. But as she drew nearer, she looked more and more like a crowned princess of the seas. No ship could have seemed more proud, except one of those square-riggers which used to go flying like white clouds across the ocean. She passed us so near on our starboard beam that she loomed almost over us, and we gazed silently up into her sails. At almost the same time we tacked, swung across the wind, and fell away to port. And now she showed us her stern, and we could see how her sails were set. They were "wing and wing" or, as the mate used to say, "wung out": that is, with the spanker to starboard, mainsail to port, and foresail and jibs hardly drawing, because of being cut off from the wind by the other sails. Even our own sails, when we had had them set that way, had not seemed so much like wings. She reminded me of a gull spreading out its wings to fly up from the water. The very lines and curves of the sails interlaced with each other, and the farther away she sailed, the more like some huge sea bird she became.

The sun made a vast stretch of gold. Soon after she had passed us, she dipped into that burning sea. First her sails grew bright with the sunlight, and then, as she sailed farther and farther into the heart of the blaze, they melted away into the sun. When we looked, there seemed to be not a vestige of sail upon her. Her handsome hull we could see perfectly, black in the mirror of gold. Even her masts were clearly outlined, her very crosstrees. But she was stripped of canvas; the sun had stolen it. She was no more than a skeleton, a weird phantom ship.

As we watched, we saw her draw out of that enchanted part of the sea. Slowly she became real again; slowly her sails appeared. First they were bright gold with reflected light, then only flushed with it; and then they were snowy once more. By this time she was tiny in the distance. At last she disappeared — into Lunenberg, the skipper thought.

This was the most perfect weather of the whole trip. The alluring hills grew brighter as the sun mounted, until they were like precious jewels in a setting of incredibly blue sky. The sea sparkled with the sun, and it, too, was bluer than on any day before. Again I was dazzled by the hugeness and the wideness of the sun-path here on the sea. The brilliant splotch of gold seems to spread out boundlessly. It is much brighter, too, than I have ever seen it on an inland lake, as though each tiny salt-crystal were reflecting the rays a thousand times. Millions, millions of sparks, leaping up from that blueness, breaking into showers of fire!

Where the sky was clear, it was a very deep blue. There

were banks of massive white clouds on the horizon, although the zenith was entirely free of them. These cast down deep shadows which cooled the green fire of the hills here and there, gliding over them slowly. We were running nearer and nearer now. The skipper had located us and determined where Lahave was. We had passed it, as the cook had said, and were wheeling about to find it; running back the way we had come, but much nearer to the coast than before, so that it seemed different, and much more beautiful. All the time, though we were running down the coast, we were drawing closer and closer to it, and the hills looked more and more verdurous. What a contrast to the vacancy of boundless ocean which we had had before us a few days back!

* * *

THERE seemed to be a great many small fishermen hereabout. We didn't actually pass any close, but we counted seven or eight off on the horizon. We would be looking at one sail, a tiny peak fretting the skyline, when someone would catch sight of another. But they were all so far away and so hard to see that our eyes went crazy after a while, so that all we could see was miniature sails.

There was hardly time for staring at them, for we were now nearing Lahave. We could see a deep, narrow indentation in the shore line, bounded on each side by hills sloping down into the sea — no more than two arms of green land, clasping the bay within. It looked like a very narrow opening for a schooner of our size to sail through, and I wondered what could be done, supposing there were an adverse wind. I climbed up in the rigging two or three times more before we reached the opening, feeling extremely glad, deep down, to have retrieved that privilege. The hills and the stretch of blue harbor within looked, of course, lovelier than ever from so high, and I stayed up at the crosstrees, watching our progress toward it, for quite a long time. Although we seemed to be so near, we were as yet easily two miles away, the mate said. Suddenly we heard the booming of surf on a small rock-bound islet to the starboard of the entrance. We could see the great white crests rise up and up, toweringly, like foam-castles, then dash furiously up the bar a way, then subside into themselves with a crash and a dull roar. And all this two miles away!

The mate and I fell to talking. We leaned over the starboard bulwarks watching the surf, and talked mainly about swimming. The mate said: "Well, kin you swim, Barbara?"

"Oh yes, mate," said I, "I swim a lot. I believe I could swim from here over to that island."

Two miles?" He looked at me incredulously. "Well, perhaps not quite," I yielded. "But almost. How are you on swimming?"

"I can't swim a stroke," said Bill. "Y' see, I hain't never had no chance."

"But it strikes me," said I, "that anyone who's a sailor *ought* to be able to."

"Well, ye're right, I reckon," said he. "But I never been shipwrecked yit. 'N' I'm goin' t' resign afore long, too!" And his eyes sparkled, as usual, at his joke.

He began telling about his working abilities. "You know, I do twice as much work's any other man aboard here. They all act 's though they was skeered to death t' get their hands dirty. Why, 'f I didn't work with 'em — 'f I didn't sooge the deck 'n' paint the bulwarks — there'd not be a stroke o' work done here. There's a thousand little jobs that no one 'll ever do 'ceptin' myself. Remember that day when you come down t' the schooner 'n' I was sewin' that outer jib? Well, the boys got the afternoon off, and I could 'ave, too, if I'd ast; but w'at did I do? I stayed aboard, like a blinkin' fool, and worked all afternoon on that jib. Well, 't would have never got done 'f I hadn't done it."

Evidently the mate's head was still running strong on knots, for, after a little, he got himself a strand of rope, and fell to tying it up in all the ways he could think of. I asked him how Richardson was at tying knots. Bill replied about as I expected: "Oh, Dick! he can't tie two half-hitches and git 'em right."

I was eager to show him *something* about string that he didn't know, but I felt that this was impossible. At last I had an idea: "Do you know cat's-cradle, mate?" "Cat's-cradle? No." I ran down into the cabin and hunted up a bit of string. For as much as a half-hour we were taking it off each other's hands. I succeeded in amusing the mate by it; and to me it seemed a more interesting game than ever before. It is perfect to play on shipboard, between watches.

Then we fell to talking about boats — small ones, such as canoes and rowboats. Said he: "Well, I tell you, I niver was very strong on canoes. I'm skeered of 'em. Too tipsy for me! I tell you, I wouldn't go out in one in rough weather 'f you paid me." And I told him what fun Daddy and I used to have on Sunapee and Ossipee, battling in the white canoe the strongest gales that came.

"But, of course," said I, "there you never have any weather that's dangerous. You never have weather anything like what we had a few days ago."

The talk somewhat broke up as we neared the harbor. Mate Bill had never been to Bridgewater, and it struck him, no less than me, as very lovely country. The bright green of the hills rose up, dominating everything, and reaching down those two almost human arms to clasp the blue waters of the bay. I shall never, never forget the loveliness of the entrance to that river as we came directly outside it and began to swing in. The breeze seemed to reach quite a distance up into the bay, and we sailed easily before it, the sails full and steady. At every inch of our progress the landscape changed. Now we would look up the river, where it disappeared around a bend; then back out at the sea, where there seemed to be two horizons — first the edge of our own bay, clasped with those hill-arms, then the horizon of the sea itself, stretching away outside, blue and boundless.

Perhaps you have seen pictures of the Mediterranean Sea, or of harbors in Italy, and wondered at the incredible greenness of the hills, the blueness of the water. Here it was the same: the hills were so gorgeously bright, and shone in such crystal contrast to the brilliant sea and bay, that you just couldn't believe it was real. Such color could not exist! Green and blue flames, mingling together, yet sharply outlined and distinguished. Those hills were like an emerald crown for the sea. At one place where we looked back at the sea which we were leaving so fast, that boundless mass of color shone bravely between two islands — small islands, just out at the edge of the bay. Being shadowed by higher hills, they looked dark, almost as though spruce-forested. In contrast, that glowing stretch of sea looked brighter, bluer, than ever.

THERE was quite a breeze in here; there were even whitecaps glistening now and then. The skipper was in high hopes that the breeze would reach clear up the river to the anchoring ground, so that we shouldn't have to be towed. He wanted to progress as far up the river that night as possible. But when we hailed some men who were working on an anchored three-master, they said that the wind didn't reach up far, and that the tide was running out "agin" us. The skipper decided to stick to it as long as he could. I went up in the rigging again. I looked down upon a sea of billowing green hills, inset with the sapphires of the various pools which formed parts of the great bay; also, upon more wind and waves than I had realized there were. Then I saw a little power boat, looking like no more than a very large canoe with an engine and a great dark red sail, scudding rapidly out toward us. The man who was running it hailed the skipper, who had been looking down over the starboard bulwarks, ever and again taking the wheel himself. "Want a pilot up the river?" "No, I guess not," shouted our skipper in return. As for me, I felt more than ever elated in my high station on the crosstrees, especially since I was looking down over nothing but beautiful country. The little power boat with its dark red sail looked so much like a child's toy from up there that I couldn't resist waving to the man in its stern. But either he didn't see me or else he had his hands full running the boat, for I got no return.

A little farther on a small launch sped up to our side and asked the same question, promptly receiving the same answer from the captain. But still farther on, when the hills and small emerald islands began to cut off the wind, and the sails began to flap, and we found that the tide was sweeping us down, the captain replied differently to the skipper of a tug who shouted over "Want a tug up?" "Yes, sure!"

The tug came close to the side of the *Norman D.* The skipper, a very curious-looking Dutchman, leaped aboard and shook Captain Avery warmly by the hand, after first looking him over incredulously from head to heel. "Why! If this ain't Cap'n Avery!" said he.

"True for you," said our skipper. "Glad I am t' see you, Joe."

" 'T's a bully long time since you've been up Bridgewater way — eh, Cap?"

"Hey-y-y-y-y?"

"You hain't been up this way fer a long time, Cap!"

"No, I haven't."

And the like friendly remarks went on monotonously, with extreme cheerfulness, for a long time. Nothing I could ever say would adequately describe the Dutchman. He was a huge, broad-shouldered man with a huge face and small, glistening blue eyes. He looked wild, but nevertheless kindly. He had a crazy manner of friendliness and nonchalance, and he swanked about the schooner as if he were her captain. I felt that he was extremely amiable at heart, and I was very much interested and amused by him. Incidentally, he was a lively and vigorous tobacco-chewer.

And now Richardson was to have his moment of excitement. It was this way: The towrope was attached to the tug, and Richardson was called aft by "Here, boys! Here, boys! Here, boys!" to make it fast around our two starboard mooring-posts. If he had been wise, he would have let someone else answer that call. He did it, as I thought, quite briskly and cleverly, winding the rope in a figure-of-eight formation around the two posts. But the Dutchman, who had leaped briskly back into the tug to superintend things in his swaggering way there, decided that it wasn't short enough, and he bellowed back his opinion to Captain Avery. "Take up the slack!" whooped Captain Avery. But this was not such an easy matter for Richardson. To begin with, all those fancy figure-of-eight loops which he had cast around the mooring-posts had to be untangled. He didn't seem to have a very successful time of it getting them off. I must here remark that, whenever anything was found carelessly done, it was always Richardson who was to blame. For instance, one morning when we had tacked, the bo's'n had sprung to the main sheet where it was belayed. If there had been any wind, Richardson's belaying (for, presumably, it *was* Richardson's) wouldn't have lasted long. It was very loosely tangled around the pin. In a flash the bo's'n had exclaimed: "That looks like Richardson's work! He must 'a' done that." Yes, Richardson did betray a kind of mixed-up sloppiness in his work. He had just got the figures-of-eight off the mooring-posts and begun to haul up the slack in the towrope, when Captain Avery, irritated beyond endurance by his slowness, thundered out: "Hurry up there, Richardson! Hurry up! Hurry! Quick! Quick! Blast you, Richardson! Quick!" in such an appalling voice that Richardson worked desperately, getting in the slack. I never saw a man cast figures-of-eight with such rapidity, and he did not stop until there was enough rope on the posts to have held the entire Presidential Range a mile above ground. Then he went forward, the skipper glowering at him.

Now the captain of the tug had come aboard again, along with one of the tug's crew — a wild, glaring-eyed youth, slender as a nail and very dark. The two skippers began talking in a very friendly way, calling each other — apparently after the Dutch or Nova Scotian fashion — "Cap." The glaring youth hung around for a while, but, finding that the two had nothing in particular to communicate to him, he returned, after one inquisitive glance, to his work aboard the tug.

We were now gliding smoothly and rather briskly up into the harbor. The river widened out gradually, with ever and again beautiful glimpses back at the emerald islets and the sea, or up ahead into the hills, down among which the water flowed, looking bright sapphire blue. After what seemed a very short time, the tug left us in the loveliest landlocked harbor imaginable. The green hills dipped away in a wide sweep and circle to right and left, clasping the blue bay, whose waters seemed to murmur with the rush of the tide. On each side, and lying down beneath the hills, were towns, very small and elfin from this distance. The masses of close-set white and gray houses, with now and then a large red barn looming in the greenness of fields and hills, completed one's idea of a landlocked Italian harbor. The fields were bright sunny green, by contrast with the more vivid emerald of the hills. Two small islands over on the west side of the bay looked mysterious and uninhabited, as though they sheltered pirate treasure. One of them seemed to have a fairly good landing-beach on our side of it; but this beach, though smooth and gradual, appeared to be covered with some mysterious dark substance which I could by no means understand.

We were far from being the only schooner there. Indeed, it seemed like quite a busy little country seaport. A small three-master was lying close in at one of the wharves belonging to the western town; a shapely little schooner with a black hull. Others lay scattered at anchor around the edges of the harbor — some of them being used, and others (among them a dismantled two-master, one of whose topmasts was gone) in a disused state. The *Norman D.* was, however, by far the largest and loveliest of the schooners there, and we entered that enchanted circle of water feeling as proud and lovely as a white-robed queen. The tug left us near the middle of the bay, but slightly nearer the western edge. Down went our mudhook, with a magical and melancholy splash.

Here I must confess a great weakness of mine, in a moment of which I submitted ingloriously to human nature. I felt, in the presence of the queer, domineering Dutch skipper, as if I should rather like to show that I wasn't an "ornery street gal," and that I had some small ability as a sailor. I began to be just as helpful as I could possibly manage. I bustled and ran around after Mate Bill, who was getting the sail-stops out. He got those coils of rope, each about ten feet long, out of one of the small after hatchways, and each of us took an armful and went forward, distributing them. He would leave a certain number by the spanker boom, ready for use, and then another bundle by the mainsail boom; the first bundle went to the foresail. The sails were still up, having been left in order to help our progress up the river; and the mate simply tossed the sail-stops over the boom so that they lay across it, each end trailing on the deck, ready to receive the sails when they should be let down. Together we fitted out the foresail and mainsail booms; then the mate, having something else to do, left me to finish the spanker. I did so, at least as far as I could reach, and then he came aft and placed the stops across the overhanging end.

* * *

ALL the time the mate was talking in earnest, agitated tones about the skipper of the tug. He certainly was a character worth some small consideration. The mate didn't approve of him at all. He struck Bill as a snob, somehow, much too proud to talk to a common sailor; indeed, he hadn't said a word to the mate in all the time he was on the schooner. And, as Richard H. Dana, Jr., says: "When the voyage is at an end, you do as you please; but so long as you belong to the same vessel, you must be a shipmate to him on shore, or he will not be a shipmate to you on board." And Bill had a delicate streak of sensitiveness.

The mate thought that the skipper of the tug was very vulgar because he chewed tobacco so much and so heartily — he thought the same, as a matter of fact, about Captain Avery himself — and he went on somewhat in this way:

"Now, here's how it is with me. I don't approve o' such things's chewin' tobacker, drinkin', 'n' so on. I don't approve of 'em, 'n' I never can. I used t' chew a little when I was a young lad and first went t' sea, 'cause I didn't know better. But I give it up afore long. 'N' as fer smokin' — well, I smoke a cigarette now and then, but not as a stiddy thing. 'N' drinkin'? Well, I'm not a boasting man, but I'll tell you that I was never drunk once in all my life. Now, that's a pretty good record fer a man that's lived as rough as I have, and been t' sea fifteen year. And I've never, in all my born days, bought more than one bottle o' whisky.

"But Bob, m' brother, him'd get drunk ivery day if he had th' chance. As it is, he gets drunk every time he goes ashore. I talk and talk and argue 'bout it with him, but it never does no good. Y' can't drum any reason into that lad. He beats all!"

So we talked together — or, at least, I listened and the mate talked — until we dropped anchor in the midst of that peaceful bay. It was now getting toward sunset, and the old man wanted to go ashore to the little sleeping town in order to telephone for a tug to pull us up to Bridgewater in the morning. The mate lowered a small, light flat-bottomed skiff which had been hoisted just beneath the larger dory on the davits, and concealed by it. (In fact, I had not noticed it before.) It was lowered, brought around to the port side of the schooner, and tied just beneath the taffrail. Then a stout ladder was brought, put down the side of the ship, and made fast. I was eager to watch the skipper descend this vertical ladder, as well as to see him try to row the little skiff. The cook, probably eager to see him make a miscue and get a wetting, came sedately out of the galley and stood watching wickedly.

"Are you going alone, sir?" queried the mate.

"Yes, I gesso, Bill."

Secretly I had hopes of being allowed to accompany him, not having had my feet off the *Norman D.* for ten days; but the captain said nothing about it, and I said nothing. The moment of excitement was arriving. I imagine that the whole crew craned their necks from wherever they were, to see the old man fall into the waters of the Lahave River. The cook now had an I-wish-to-heaven-you'd-get-drowned look on his face. The captain asked the mate if the oarlocks were all right, and the mate descended himself, to see. They were, and the oars were put into place. Everything was in readiness. Then down went the captain, grasping the rungs desperately with his horny, trembling old hands. It looked as if everything were going all right. The mate held the painter of the skiff, ready to cast off as soon as the old man was ready, and he was holding the boat cleverly just beneath the ladder. But the skipper had not reckoned on the small, almost invisible heaves which are constantly taking place in the mouth of that river, where the water is influenced both by the tide and by the current of the river itself. Just as he was about to step into the boat, one of those smooth waves came along, sweeping the boat from beneath his feet. "Look out fer that swell, sir!" shouted the mate. The old man paid not the slightest heed, but went right on, stepping off into the boat just as that wave occurred. It disturbed his balance: and he staggered, then sprawled down into the boat just as one leg trailed in the water up to the knee. Then he regained himself, got at the oars, caught the painter as the mate threw it down, and pushed off.

He was used to rowing, all right, but the tide and the current bothered him considerably. He was swept downstream so fast that he had to head much farther upstream than he wanted to. At last he landed on a sort of beach. The mate made the remark, when he started, that he was "weaker 'n a cat."

SO odd a thing now took place among the crew that I was glad I had stayed aboard. The sails had been lowered and snugly furled, and now the crew seemed to think that there was nothing under the sun to do. They all came aft in a body, including the cook, and stood around on the poop deck, sitting on the deckhouse, chinning and making merry. The audacity of it was very amusing. When the old skipper was aboard no one ever came aft except when called, or to take his trick at the helm. But now all rules were off, and they seemed to take a defiant pleasure in being where they weren't supposed to be. Their talk ran mainly on the skipper, and they said some tremendously insulting things. The cook, through it all, pretended great authority, standing there in a way which made me think he was trying very hard to look dignified, and nodding his head grimly every now and then.

"I wisht he had fallen in — really," said the bo's'n, in a mournful voice.

"We'd 'a' been well rid o' that rascal," said the cook.

" 'N' say, Bob, didja see that guy from the tug?" said Roy. "So that's the kind o' friends the old man has, is it?"

"He'd 'a' won the champeenship of spitting," stated Bob.

"I told you," interposed the cook, "he's known all over Nova Scotia fer his low-down rascality."

" 'N' fer interferin' in *your* business, I suppose."

"Interferin 's no word fer it. Say, you know — " And then came, for the hundredth time, the tale of how the Chinese cook had chased Captain Avery ashore with a drawn cutlass when he had come forward to see the galley. This sort of talk went on for a long time, with the cook interposing now and then to call Captain Avery "cussed old wretch," and "p'ison divil," and so on, at a great rate; and with the mate standing by the taffrail, looking wicked and piratical, with that suppressed smile in his face and that black twinkle in his eyes. The bo's'n, too, was "full of it" that evening, and every now and then one of his mocking calls would ring out over the waters of the Lahave, much louder and bolder than ever before.

Presently the mate and I drew more or less apart from the others. "Say, Barbara," said Bill, "how'd you like a row in that little skiff when the old man comes back, if 't ain't too late?"

"Oh, that would be splendid."

"Kin you row?"

"Try me and see!"

"Well, you can row, then, and, if 't ain't too dark, we'll go out."

"All right. But say, mate, are the boys going ashore tonight?"

"Yes, I reckon they are, if they can get the chance. We'll give 'em the skiff when we get back."

"Are you going ashore?"

"No, I reckon not."

By this time the sun was nearing the horizon, spreading a gorgeous russet glow over there, and looking like a great ball of scarlet fire. Suddenly there was a loud hail from near where the old man had beached the skiff. All of us thought it was he; it sounded unmistakably like his harsh whoop. "Here, boys! Here, boys! Here, boys!" said the bo's'n shrilly. "Don't you want us to swim over and git you?"

But the mate silenced him, with a mild oath, and answered the hail with one loud "Hallo-o-o-o-o!" Then there was a dead silence. The crew was staring. The cook was the first one to speak: "I would be glad if that was the old man's death-whoop," said he. These words fell from the mouth of the sinister little old man in an icy way, sounding like a death-knell indeed. The bo's'n was next, and he said: "What's that? Go buy a package o' cigarettes!" And next the mate: "Oh, shame, to mock the poor old fellow like that! I wouldn't talk that way about him for worlds; not me!" "Huh!" said the cook. "Cap'n Avery jaws me about smokin' a few decent little cigarettes, 'n' then — w'at does he do? He goes 'n' chaws *tobacker*!"

By this time we had all decided that it wasn't the captain at all, and we began talking again as merrily as ever. The mate was looking rather stern now, or, at least, trying to, but something in his eye and the corners of his mouth told me that he enjoyed the jokes of the crew. Then a little speck was descried off through the dark, and, behold! it was the skipper returning, rowing back in the same feeble way. He was welcomed with quite a burst of subdued mocks from the bo's'n, and then the crew slunk away forward and disappeared in a very businesslike way. Even the haughty little cook went forward to the galley pretty fast.

* * *

"DON'T you think it's too late for us to go out in the skiff?" I asked the mate. It was now almost dark, and the glow in the west had faded to a deep russet.

"Oh, there's no reason why we can't go out a little," said Bill, who was evidently quite eager about the idea.

A few moments afterward the old man had come in close, the mate had caught the thrown painter, and the captain had scrambled out of the skiff and up the ladder. "Now, Barbara!" said the mate, with a cunning wink at me. Instantly I had started down the ladder. "Won't you be cold with nothing but that jumper on?"

"No, I think not," said I. I climbed down the ladder and got successfully into the boat.

"Do you want to row, Barbara?"

"Surely, mate, unless you do."

"All right, then — you row."

He cast the painter down to me. I caught it, holding the ladder with the other hand. Down came the mate, and we pushed off. It gave me very delightful sensations to come down that ladder. It struck home upon my piratical senses that it must be very much like the sort of ladder by which buccaneers would board other ships. Even going down instead of up, I had the feeling of boarding the ship of an enemy. But my ideas changed when I felt the oars securely in my hands, and I decided to show the mate a little brisk rowing. Feeling quite in my own element, I struck out. The little skiff was so much lighter and happier than the heavy old tubs I am accustomed to rowing that, under my tremendous strokes, we shot along amazingly, in spite of the powerful river current which had seemed to trouble the old man. I can't explain to you the delight I had in being in a small boat again and having oars grasped firmly in my hands. It seemed strange, too, to see the little waves so very near me. I leaned back with all my weight upon the oars, bringing them down together in strong, quick rhythm. How lightly the skiff danced on! I knew that progress at this rate would draw comment from Bill sooner or later, and, indeed, I didn't have long to wait: "Say, you sure can row good, Barbara!"

"Well, yes — I'm pretty well used to it. I've rowed quite a lot before."

We agreed to go over towards the place where the captain had landed, but farther upstream, so that we should have a good chance to see the small three-masted schooner which was lying close in to the wharf there. There was quite a wind added to the current; I felt a pleasant resistance, and heard the whispering chuckle of waves beneath the bow. I had been rowing some minutes very briskly, not thinking of anything in particular, and more or less watching the water. Suddenly the mate said: "The schooner looks pretty from here, don't she, Barbara?" I raised my head and looked back. The *Norman D.* lay there, in the midst of those unstill waters, like a dream — a thought. Ten times lovelier she seemed than ever before. She raised her head quietly from that small round bay, and shone, in her whiteness, like a beautiful ghost. At one moment she dominated the entire ring of hills like a snow-capped mountain looming from a sea of dark foothills and spruce forests; at another she only blended softly and quietly with the water, like a wraith of the sea; again, she was a drifting sea gull, or a snowy albatross with dark wings. By the magical influence of the dusk, she was quivering and unsteady, like a mirage. And soon she was no more than a lovely white shadow — a flicker — a whim of the twilight. Whatever she was or might be, all images of piracy left me at the sight of her, lying calm and innocent in the dusk.

Not until all these thoughts had passed through me did I answer the mate. "Pretty? I should say she is!"

* * *

BUT now we had almost reached the other schooner. I hadn't ceased my vigorous rowing, though, in wonder of the *Norman D.*, it had considerably abated.

"Are you getting tired, Barbara?"

I nearly smiled. If he had known the way I had rowed around and about Lake Sunapee, in a boat which took twice as much strength as this one merely to keep under way — ! "Me? No, mate. I don't get tired so easily as that!" And I gradually speeded up again. The other schooner, the small three-master, seemed, in the soft darkness, much more like a pirate craft than that snow-lily of a *Norman D.* She had a slender, graceful black hull with a band of yellow around it below the bulwarks, and her name in yellow letters. Alas! I have forgotten what it was. She was a dainty little vessel; the mate, too, said so.

"Well, where would you like to go now, Barbara?"

"What do you say about going over to the island on the other side of the bay?"

"Are you sure you can row that far?"

"Oh, certainly, certainly."

"You don't want me to take her?"

"Not unless you want to."

Here, you see, I made use of this pleasure excursion to get a glimpse of that mysterious little island about which I had become so curious. I wanted to see what that dark beach really was. We crossed the bow of the *Norman D.* at a slashing rate. (Both of us raised our eyes and saw her huge, high jibboom looming about us, seeming to point at the sky itself.) We neared the island; closer and closer we drew in, until we could hear the breeze whispering in its trees. It loomed darksomely. It is one of my lasting regrets that I didn't have the chance to land and do some true exploration there, in the approved piratical fashion. I am sure that considerable treasure might have been found. But by this time it was getting pretty dark, and we couldn't see where we were going. The mate was afraid to let me land, because we didn't know the place, and we couldn't see where rocks were. But closer and closer I drew in, rowing very slowly now. I could see jagged rocks thrusting up from the water close to the shore. Now we could almost *feel* that uncanny dark island, like the breath of a ghost upon our cheeks.

Ahead was that mass of darkness which I once thought had been a beach. Now I still thought that it was a beach, covered with seaweeds. But when I saw what it really was, I was so surprised that I forgot where I was going. It was nothing but a huge, long shelf of dark rock, sloping down gradually from the woods to the sea, almost at the grade of a beach, and almost as smooth as a paved street. It was covered thickly with massive seaweeds, some of them, I could see in the half-light, as much as six feet long; a dense, dark shroud of them, spread like a mermaid carpet over that great rock, with the waves gently lifting and stirring those which overhung into the sea.

This was the final impression of the island. And it served to implant that little place very firmly in my memory. I made a deep resolve that, if I should ever chance to go up Lahave way again, I would at any cost visit that island. We ought to go together there, Alan, with our shovels and picks over our shoulders, in the search for treasure. Can't you see us doing it? Fifty-fifty! Only we *must* pick out a sailing vessel to go in. Don't you think so? Can you conceive of any earthly pleasure in going on a pirate expedition in a steamer? I can't. In such a case you always want to go in the way you suppose the pirates themselves went. The nearer you can do it to the way they did it, the nearer success you will be. That is a secret which few treasure-hunters know, and you had better keep it fairly close. Such secrets must not be revealed to the world.

Mate Bill and I talked little during this cruise. What we did say was mostly about Bridgewater, and schooners, and the sea, and the old man, and the steward; and I said some things about Lake Sunapee, canoes, rowboats, sailboats, swimming, fishing, and so on. It was very quiet, almost whispered talk, for we were somehow under the influence of the night, and of the beauty of the little landlocked harbor. Also, we were awed by the queenliness of the *Norman D.*, towering there so white that you fancied she was in full moonlight while the rest of the world wasn't. The water beneath her heel and forefoot was black, very black; yet we could somehow detect brighter shadows moving about and blending into it.

"Isn't she a very good-looking schooner, mate, for one of her size?"

"Yes, I think she is. She's one o' the best-looking three-masters I've ever seen. But she's too high forrard. Now, 'f she was just a little lower forrard, or a bit higher aft, she'd be just right. The stern of any ship ought to be higher than the forrard part, to look right."

Bill was, in all probability, right about that. But she was so beautiful and quiet there that it seemed almost profane to disturb her by such minute criticism. No more was said until we had got very near her. Because she was at anchor, the side lights (which, by the way, I had so faithfully watched being lit every night while we were under way) were not lit, but three or four very small, bright riding lights were gleaming, up fairly high in the rigging, at bow and stern, mysterious in the darkness, hovering like fireflies with perpetual lights above the vast white hulk.

Again the mate broke the silence: "When you go back to the schooner, Barbara, go close under her stern, will you? There's a spot there I want to look at."

"All right, mate."

"But you'll have to be careful to allow fer the current."

"I guess I can manage it."

Quickly and, I think, rather skillfully, I guided the little skiff under the counter of the *Norman D*. Not until then could we really see how fast the current was running. It was sweeping past the schooner at a tremendous rate. The shadow of the overhanging stern made the water uncanny and green there. And the gigantic rudder hung there, motionless, dark and awful in its immense curves. I liked to think how often that same rudder had guided the *Norman D*. through tempestuous waters.

The mate looked at a place on the bottom where the wood seemed to be worn and frayed. Then we pushed on and drew up at the foot of the ladder. There was another boat dancing there, tied by its painter. What could it mean? We made our own skiff fast and climbed up. I felt more than ever like a pirate boarding a ship, as I climbed up that crude vertical ladder with the mate following me. I could almost feel a cutlass between my teeth. But when I remembered the loveliness of the lonely white schooner as she had looked from a little way off in the bay, this feeling vanished entirely.

* * *

THE next thing was to see who were our guests. The bo's'n greeted us, and said in a playful whisper: "The old man's got callers." Next we heard harsh, racking, scraping sounds from below. "What on earth — ?" said I. "The old man's playing his gramophone." Well, thought I, there goes one of the cook's statements! He evidently *isn't* too stingy to use the needles, after all. He was playing some horrible talking record, and he seemed quite to be enjoying himself, for I heard loud bursts of whooping laughter every now and then, followed by the happy giggles of some female voice. I could resist no longer, and I stomped heavily down the after doorway of the cabin, striding briskly through, glancing curiously to right and left as I passed, and then stomping out the forward door. I beheld very strange things. The captain was sitting beside the gramophone, laughing and beaming all over, and in the two rooms of the cabin was quite an audience of old and young, with two or three giggling girls and children. I must confess that I resented such an intrusion into the *Norman D*. I felt that these people could not belong to the adventures that had surrounded me for the past several days. No; they were landsmen — they had no business here.

I fled forrard, in company with Mate Bill and my shipmate. The cook was in the galley, and we gathered there, a jolly company, and had a regular "go" of it. The boys — Richardson, Irish Bill, Roy, and Bob — had taken possession of the skiff and started briskly ashore. Trust them to take the first opportunity! The cook was disgusted with them, as he always was. He said it was ridiculous that four full-grown men should try to jam themselves into that skiff, built for not more than two. In his day such foolishness wouldn't have been allowed. This deserting all duty and running ashore at the first chance made him sick, he said. Then he fell to arguing with the mate as to which could do the worse things to the old man, and which could strike the harder blow. The mate insisted that the steward couldn't make him feel anything, and the cook said he had made many a better man feel a great deal. This talk continued for a long time. Among other things, we heard once more the tale of how the Chinese cook had chased Captain Avery ashore with a drawn cutlass, and the tale of how the cook was seasick in his bunk for ten days, and how the quart of cold tea cured him. Those two were his favorites. After that discussion was ended, and the landlubbers had gone back to land, the three of us went aft, leaving the cook to shut up the galley for the night. There was a little more friendly but insignificant talk with the mate, out in the frosty starlight; then we turned in.

For about the first time during that whole trip, we slept steady — that is, with no rolling. Although at first I missed that cradling motion, I slept as soundly as ever.

*　*　*

IN the morning I got out on deck early. The harbor and the hills around it looked, by broad daylight, twice as lovely as before. How blue that water, and how like ancient towns the two little villages, lying there amid those green, green hills!

A little way up the stream was a sort of thing which looked like a large, fat bell buoy. I was sure I hadn't seen it in the evening. I asked the mate about it, and "Blamed if I know" was all I got. Captain Avery didn't understand it, either. All of a sudden the top of it threw forth a glorious shower of red sparks, accompanied by a long *fiz-z-z-z-z-z!* and the thing, whatever it was, started slowly churning down the river, lifting its head high like some monstrous ancient dragon or a crocodile of some extinct and forgotten species. As it came closer and closer, with a curious gliding motion, we saw that it was a sort of raft with an engine, laden with mud and clay. A mud-scow!

Two small tugs came churning downstream. The old man hailed them both through his long speaking-trumpet, and asked each if it were the tug that was to tow him up. Both replied that others were coming down shortly. Meanwhile the mate had started mixing up a dark green paint for the waterways, and the captain was standing over his shoulder, pestering the life out of him, and telling him that the color wasn't dark enough, or that it wasn't bright enough, and that it needed a touch of this, and that, and the other. The mate was mighty glad when he got the bucket prepared to the satisfaction of the old man. (Incidentally, he insisted that there was altogether too much of the color mixed for the waterways, and the mate obstinately persisted that there wasn't too much. When the old man got out of the way for a moment, he repeated slyly to me his former statement that if the old fellow could have his way "he'd make one can o' paint go for the hull ship.") He took the can down by the port waterways and started painting, but the old man came up and said something critical about it. This was the last straw. The mate deliberately laid down his brush, left the paint-can, and strode over to where I was sitting, without so much as another look at the captain. Then said he: "P'isonous old wretch! Always interferin', as usual! Well, all I can say is, if he wants me to take it easy, I sure will." And he did.

But now the crew were gathering up forward to tell their adventures to the mate and the cook. I wanted to be in on that, and I went skipping up forward, too. Bob was the chosen orator of the party, and he began, with strange chuckles and squeaks and scrapes and rasps, to tell the tale.

"How many new wimmenfolks did you pick up?" asked the cook.

"I dunno why," replied the bo's'n, "but all the wimmenfolk seemed t' be mighty feared of us. We was goin' along, when we come up behind a woman with a big basket, 'n' she took one good look behind her, 'n' then ducked into the first doorway. When we passed, we looked back, 'n' there she was agin, walkin' behind us. Well, a little further on we come up to two girls walkin' along. 'N' they did jist the same thing. They ducked right into the first doorway, 'n' waited awhile, till we went by. 'N' then, when we looked back agin, there they was, comin' along behind."

"Pshaw!" said the mate, "you'll get all the gals in Bridgewater so skeered of us that when I go ashore they won't come anywhere near me. I don't go ashore like that, skeering all the wimmenfolk out o' their wits. I go ashore like a gen'leman, I do. W'at do you 'xpect, goin' ashore lookin' like bums, you?"

"Say, Bill," interposed Bob, again, "you're no more a gen'leman when y' go ashore 'n I am. I got a new suit, I have, 'n' new shoes, too."

"So have I," said Roy, "and a brand-new four-in-hand tie."

"Me, too," said Richardson, " 'n' a tie-pin, too."

"Who give it to you?" said Roy.

"M' best girl."

"Humph!" said Bill, emphatically. "I can take the shine out o' you all, when I make up m' mind to 't."

* * *

BUT now events were occurring aft, and I scampered back again. A third tug was chugging its way slowly down the river, and the old man had his speaking-trumpet all ready and was mustering up his whoops to hail it. It proved to be the right tug; and the skipper shouted to the mate, up forrard, to get the mudhook up.

"Get up the mudhook, boys!" trilled out the bo's'n, in such a voice that I wonder the skipper didn't hear him. I ran forward again, at this, to see the anchor come up — something I always loved. Somehow it wasn't, this time, so ghostlike and awesome as on the day when, out of sight of land, we had hauled it up through the fog. But there is always one moment, just before the arms reach out of the water, when it reminds one of a skeleton.

The tug was now rapidly making fast on our port side. (Richardson, I noticed, stuck most carefully to his painting of the bulwarks.) When the skipper of this tug jumped aboard, I fairly caught my breath with amazement. He was exactly the same sort of man as the other tug master — wild, kindly, huge, Dutch, and another "champeen" spitter; and with the same swaggering, swanky, bossy, familiar way. He also recognized Captain Avery, and greeted him in almost the same way as the other, calling him, also, "Cap." Captain Avery recognized him, too, and again we watched the two sitting there in a most friendly way, asking each other how this person was, and that was, and whether they remembered how they once changed watchchains, and saying how glad they were to see each other again, and one asking how the voyage down was, and the other replying that "we got caught i' the fog fer a few days — wet, nasty fog, ye knaow, with a sloppy, nasty roll going."

The new arrival was even more of a champeen spitter than the other. While he was steering the schooner (for Captain Avery was so obliging as to let him steer, which the other appreciated), he would simply turn his head and spit clean and clear over the bulwarks. It was Homeric. Again the mate filled my ears with his non-approval, and he talked considerably about what a mess the fellow was making all over the deck. "He seems t' be pretty good at it, though," said Bill. "Poor old Cap'n Avery has t' go clean t' the side o' the schooner when he wants t' spit."

I was glad to be starting on this little run up the river, though I had secretly hoped to explore that mysterious island early in the morning. We went around bend after bend of the stream, always seeing new bends ahead. Sometimes we passed pine and spruce woods; sometimes there was nothing but hills; sometimes there were fields and orchards of apple trees, or country villages, or yellow and gray beaches. Once we passed a place where a small schooner was under construction. I longed to stay and examine her closely. She was a very deep-bottomed boat, not more than a hundred feet long, yet apparently destined to be a three-master. I should have loved to see her finished. A three-master of that size must look quite like a fairy ship.

It seemed no time at all before we rounded the last great curve of the river, and saw, ahead of us, Bridgewater spread out, one dense mass of houses and higher buildings, crowded together like an army. I hated to see the proud and strong *Norman D.*, her sails down and furled, being towed, pushed, dragged, hauled, up the river by such a puny, dirty tug, like a prisoner or a wrecked ship, as if she were incapable of taking care of herself; she who took care of herself so nobly when there was wind, and she had sea room!

Well, here we were at the end of the interesting part of our journey. Our piratical adventure had ended. A month before, I had had not the slightest idea that it could even begin. Three weeks before, I had only the faintest hopes; it was then like a dream somewhere in the future. Two weeks before, I had longed for it and clamored for it. And then it had suddenly become real and tangible, almost clutchable. Eleven days before, I was wild because I couldn't believe it. Ten days ago, I had started; it was real, after all! All this went through my mind quickly and silently. How mysterious is Time, and how strange in its doings — the same thing ahead of you one day, behind you the next! Here we were in Bridgewater.

The tug took us in to the wharf on the eastern side of the town, just ahead of a schooner very much like the *Norman D.* She was another three-master, with a black painted hull and ornaments, and her name in yellow letters, very fancily decorated with yellow curves and scrolls. Her name was *Hazel L. Myra*.

By the wharf were sky-high piles of lath, bound up in great bundles like shocks of corn. It was the next cargo of the *Norman D.*, all ready for New York. The wharf was dirty and disused, as was this part of the town. Three boys, street urchins in rags, came strolling by to look at the new schooner. A couple of laughing, robust farmers passed and spoke to the Captain. The day was unmercifully hot, and I felt rather weary and depressed, and longed to be out at sea again, in a good brisk sailing breeze, with the whitecaps roaring and looking like wild white warhorses.

* * *

SUDDENLY there came a faint, warm breath of wind upon my port cheek. The tug left us and chugged away, muddying the water with her propeller. Then an impulse came over me — an irresistible impulse to climb, and climb, and climb; up on to the crosstrees, up to the sky. I could no more tell you why than I could say why I knew I wanted to climb the mainmast rigging rather than any other. And this was not, strangely enough, for the sake of "showing off" to the boys and farmers. Many times I have climbed for that reason — to show that I was not a landlubber — but this was for no earthly reason at all; I simply wanted to climb. And climb I did! I went up like a cat, a squirrel. I never stopped until I reached my well-beloved crosstrees. Then I sat down, and thought and thought, looking down all the time upon the people so far below me. And I thought of them, and of how small and insignificant they were, like grains of pepper in the pepper-caster. I laughed at them proudly. And yet I was no less insignificant myself, from down there! I was only a chipmunk frisking up into the branches.

When one is sitting on the crosstrees, one is in an entirely separate world. Perhaps you feel that you're in Heaven — that is, as to position; perhaps you are a god on Olympus, looking down upon the world. However you feel, I think there is always an idea that someone ought to be on the crosstrees of the mast next to you. I don't know quite why, but I always had that sense. Then it would be entirely like a separate world: two would make a vast population. You would look across to each other, and nod, and smile, as if to say some secret that no one else knew anything about; and it would be so strange to be friendly over such a chasm! That was how the ancient Greek gods and goddesses must have felt, alone with each other on Olympus, looking down on a world so far below, and yet having a world of their own right with them. You begin to get a sense — a vague idea — of the immensity of space. It is strange what a difference sixty feet can make. It is the same on a mountain-top.

I CAME down from the mainmast crosstrees, feeling sorry to be at Bridgewater. My shipmate was in the act of scrambling over the side of the schooner. Shortly afterward he disappeared upon the country road, evidently going to find out about trains. Then the steward suggested that the mate should go ashore to get the mail, if there were any. The captain had gone ashore immediately upon touching the wharf, and the mate was free to do whatever he liked. It was agreed that he should go up to the post office, and I with him.

The mate started to change his clothes, but the steward stopped him, saying: "Oh, shucks, Bill! go as you are."

"Oh, I couldn't."

"Sure! go ahead."

"I niver yet went ashore lookin' this way. I'd be ashamed to."

"Oh, never mind, mate," said I. "You go as you are, and I'll go as I am, and we'll have a bully time of it."

Agreed. We scrambled over the side, and felt the ground beneath our feet again. It was very strange. Even when the schooner was in port and safe out of the wind, there was a feeling about her that the ground doesn't have; an air of unsteadiness. She feels like a ship always. Which the ground doesn't. At first I was puzzled. I walked slowly, because it was so strange. Presently I picked up my pace and strode on at a great rate — *but* rolling from side to side with a real sailor swagger as I walked. It wasn't put on at all; it was real. I can't describe to you how queer that was. I had always, always dreamed in a vague way about going to sea, and returning brawny, sunburned, and with a sailor walk. And at last it was true, though like a dream.

So we strode merrily along, Bill in his ragged sailor clothes, with the same hat on his head that he had worn all through the trip (except in the fog, when he had worn his sou'wester). His shirt-sleeves were rolled up, as they always were, and his shirt was unbuttoned three buttons at the neck, as it always was (except on extra hot days, when it was open clear down to his belt). I was in my gay old sailor rags, and I had on a sunburn that would have made a beach bonfire look pale. And both of us were striding along the road, side by side, with such a sailor roll, and such an I've-just-come home-from-sea,-sir look, that no one could have mistaken us for anything but sailors. I only wished I had a bit of tattooing to display, as Mate Bill had. He had a very elegant full-rigged ship on the inside of his left forearm, almost buried in brawn and brownness. He told me, with an air of pride, that it had cost him two dollars to have it put on.

If I had been walking, in silks and satins, beside the King of England, I could not have felt prouder than I did then. It was the supreme moment of my life. We pushed on, and everyone looked at us, as I knew they would. And somehow I could forget most successfully who I really was, and be neither more nor less than Mate Bill's shipmate. Lustily and rollingly we walked, and there were strange moments when, as I looked ahead at the dusty road, curving into the woods, it seemed to be waving gently up and down, just as the deck or the end of the flying jibboom had waved in our rolling days. There were times when the whole world waved up and down, making me feel quite dizzy — much more so than at any time on the schooner herself. The strangeness of solid ground! We walked, Mate Bill and I.

We crossed a bridge into the main part of the town. Here were fashionable folk everywhere. We walked steadily, looking neither to left nor right, but rolling like two ships in a high cross swell. Everyone stared. But I was not myself then at all. I didn't come of even a decent family. I was a common sailor, and Mate Bill's shipmate. I let them stare. I didn't have the smallest apology to offer, to myself or anyone else, for my appearance. I held my head high and felt proud — oh, so proud! — of walking beside Mate Bill. A common sailor was higher in rank than the King of England. I was higher in rank than the Queen of it. So there we walked, the King and the Queen — Bill brown and hearty and tattooed, I scarlet, ragged, and proud.

* * *

FOR a moment or two we paused on the bridge and leaned over the railing, looking down into the water. Then we turned to look back at the *Norman D.* where she lay on the other side of the river. That was another of those supreme moments. Now we had changed from two merry, laughing comrades, walking lustily along, looking neither to right nor left, to two shipmates, two common sailors, stopping together on the streets to spin a yarn and gossip a bit. A couple of girls passed by. They nudged each other, and giggled.

We went on, with people staring and nudging each other on all sides upon our approach. We neared the post office. It was jammed full of school children, girls, jesting boys, older women. Here was the supreme chance! We went up those small, long steps two by two, instead of one at a time, and rolled our way into the place, still looking neither to left nor right, but pushing on right lustily through the crowd. We entered, the King, the Queen — he lusty and brown, and with the heartiest, merriest, most piratical sailor face you ever saw; she scarlet as fire, ragged, and very cheerful. It was "shipmate" this, "shipmate" that, all the time; I took great pains that more than one person should hear us call each other so. We elbowed, yarning merrily, through the crowd, and it certainly did make them stare to see us striding in that way, as free and easy as if we had been sailors and shipmates all our born days. In a loud voice Bill asked if the mail had come in. It hadn't, and it wasn't due for a quarter of an hour.

While Bill was asking this, I was standing just behind him, my hands on my hips, looking as full of the sea as I could. Suddenly I became aware of a lady, tall, slender, and dressed in black from head to foot, standing near me in a corner of the room. She had a curious, small, kind face, and she smiled at me so hard that I had to give her a smile in return. No doubt she, like all the rest, thought it strange to see me with Mate Bill, who, from the exposed inside of his left forearm, was certainly a sailor. People, looking at us, would feel us entirely different from what we were. They would see a very sunburned, ragged little girl in company with a hearty sailor. That was delightful, too — especially as that same sunburned little girl was so free and gay with the sailor, so shipmate-ish; but it was not nearly so delightful as my own idea that I actually was Bill's shipmate. Anyway, I didn't care; I just didn't care.

Somehow, after I had turned my head away from the woman, something within me said that she was staring hard. I felt rather as if she shouldn't stare quite so hard. It was all right to have her look at me in surprise and smile in a friendly way — that was just what I wanted; but should she keep her eyes fixed and fixed and fixed on me like that? I couldn't resist looking again, out of the corner of my eye. She *was* staring. I dropped her another smile. Then I forced myself to forget her, and looked away.

Now Bill spoke up: "What's the use of waitin' in here fer fifteen minutes? I know I'm eager enough to get out in the air. What do you say we stroll by the river a bit, 'n' then come back later?"

"All right with me, shipmate," said I. "A little fresh air wouldn't come amiss, now you speak of it. Let's go."

I spoke this quietly enough so that no one could hear — all except the "shipmate." Then, after one parting look at the woman, who was still staring, I followed Mate Bill out through the crowd, and down the little steps two by two, and down the street, and out by the river. There we stopped and strolled back and forth, as he had suggested, and talked, and went out on the bridge to look down into the water again. Soon we went back. The woman was not there, and I felt considerably relieved about that, because something in her small, quiet, kind eyes made me feel uncomfortable. They were like winking glass beads.

* * *

MATE Bill asked, in a hearty voice: "Any mail fer th' schooner *Norman D.,* the schooner that just come in here today?"

The girl sorted out the various mail for different schooners. There seemed to be a great deal for another one, but none for us.

"That's funny," said Bill. "Huh! All that trouble fer nothin'! Well, it's been a nice walk.

It had. I didn't feel in the least disappointed about the absence of mail, but I wouldn't have missed the walk for the world.

Adventures were still to befall us. We walked along, and —

"Did you see that woman in the post office, Barbara?" said Bill.

"You mean the one who was standing over in the corner and staring?"

"Yes. That's her. Wasn't she staring, though!"

"I reckon she thought we were a couple of rowdies."

"Well, we look it."

"We certainly do, shipmate! But we look like what we are — sailors."

"I never went to town lookin' so in all m' born days."

"No, but we were just like a couple of sailors, weren't we, you and I?"

"Yes — but I don't like t' go ashore with you, lookin' so awful."

"But I like you to, shipmate. It wouldn't have been fun if you and I had dressed up. We wouldn't have been sailors then at all."

"Ssh, Barbara! That's her ahead!"

It was — it was, unmistakably, the tall black woman. We strode along until we caught up with her, which, at such a gait, we did very shortly. I gave her a brief nod and a smile of recognition as we passed; otherwise I looked neither to left nor right.

The funny part of all this was that, though I was amazingly conspicuous in my rags and tatters, with my face a bonfire of sun and sea, and such a crazy sailor roll, I still wasn't in the least embarrassed.

So we rolled past until we had gone the whole length of the long bridge and come back to the *Norman D.*'s side of the river. We were stopped by the railroad track, for a long, long freight train had started across it, going very slowly. There was nothing to do but stop and wait, and talk as best we could in the terrific din. It was a long time that we stood there; and, just as we were beginning to think that the train would never come to an end, we felt someone approaching slowly and calmly behind us, and I felt a pair of beady eyes fixed on me — someone staring. I looked around quickly, and there was "her." Now the meeting was inevitable. Someone had to say something.

"How do you do?" said she, in a calm voice.

"Hello!" said I, heartily, and "Hello!" said Bill.

Then there was a rather awkward pause.

"I thought you were a little boy," said she, finally, "until I saw your pigtails." She had a curious accent which seemed to be universal among the Nova Scotians.

"Well, perhaps I do look it," said I. "We came up on the schooner — just got in this morning."

"Are ye from Yankeeland?" said she, looking at me curiously.

"I am," said I. "From Connecticut."

"And you say you came up on a schooner?"

"Yes, the *Norman D.*"

"Hm! That must have been fun. Did you enjoy it?"

"I'll say!"

"And you?" she said, turning to Bill. "Are you the captain?"

"No, first mate," said Bill, heartily enough.

"Mate," I echoed.

Another pause. Then: "Were you the only girl aboard?"

"Yes, I was, thank Heaven!" said I.

"You were glad not to have anyone else with you?"

"Indeed yes. But, say: don't you want to walk down with us and see the *Norman D?* She's mighty pretty!"

"No, I can't now."

"Well, you'll find her there for quite a long time, if you ever want to see her."

"About three weeks," said Bill.

"Thank you," said she.

The train had now gone past, and we three stepped along in company. Before many steps Bill and I passed her. She minced sedately along a short way, and then, with a final glassy look and a friendly wave of her hand, she disappeared into a little old house. Bill and I quietly returned to the schooner and climbed aboard.

* * *

THERE we found quite a state of excitement. The steward was hopping up and down the deck on one leg and saying: "The old man wants t' see you, Barbara. You better go aft 'n' see w'at he wants. I think the custom-house man is here." Aft I went, and I had to open up my hand-baggage, and to show my birth-certificate. The old man, by the way, had gone for the mail, and had evidently got it during the time when Bill and I were waiting outside. My certificate was among it.

Out on deck, everyone had letters, and they were reading them to each other. The mate took his away in a corner and spent a very long time over them. Then he told me that they were from his wife. "I got seven letters from her when we was in New Haven," said he.

And now a sad event was happening in the crew: for

Richardson was resigning. He scrubbed up, put on shore clothes, and finally went aft to the captain — probably to get his wages. He returned forrard with beaming contentment.

"I guess we weren't good enough to you, Dick," said Roy, mournfully.

"Oh, you fellows were all mighty good to me," said Richardson, almost in tears. Then he hopped off and went ashore to catch a train.

How many times I scrambled up and down the rigging, I couldn't tell. I didn't know exactly why I did it, but something was telling me that it was mighty near my parting with the *Norman D.*, and, though I was likely to climb to other crosstrees in my life, I shouldn't have much more chance to swing my legs on those of the schooner which had brought me to Nova Scotia.

It was Saturday. At last my shipmate returned aboard, and said that we shouldn't be able to get a train down until Monday. So we had the prospect of another day in Bridgewater. We decided to stay at a hotel, for we were tired of hearing the captain's complaints about sleeping on the couch; also, the charm of the schooner was lost when we were not under way. For the first time during the whole trip, I put on ladylike clothes, and appeared in the midst of the crew again. They stared like so many fish. The mate said, in a voice which sounded a little wistful: "But you didn't dress up that way when you went ashore this mornin'!"

I hoped his feelings weren't hurt. I said: "No, I didn't, because I thought it would be more fun walking through the streets looking like born sailors and shipmates."

"Well, I think I like you better in your good clothes," said he.

"Oh, NO!" I protested, in frank disappointment.

"Well, perhaps not," he yielded. "You were all right as a little sailor boy, anyhow."

The Voyage of the Norman D.

So we went off ashore. I didn't realize it at the time, but that was my last glimpse of Mate Bill as he is and ought to be. The truly last time I saw him, it was not Mate Bill at all.

We found a good hotel and deposited our luggage. Then we went out for a walk. We picked the back roads of Bridgewater and headed as much for open country as we could. The Nova Scotian people are more friendly than any I have ever seen. Everyone nodded and smiled and said "Good day!" to us, as though we had lived there all our lives. As we came out upon a long country road that led out toward a rather high hill, we passed a house where an old, sweet-looking man was mowing the lawn. We had been picking and examining the Nova Scotian wildflowers, and as soon as the old man saw that, he left his lawn-mower where it was and ran off into the back yard for a moment. When he came back he had a great bunch of pansies of gorgeous velvety colors, brighter and glossier than any I have ever seen. He gave them at once to me, saying: "I see you were lookin' fer flowers, so I brought you some. You don't need to thank me, 'cause I'm so deef I couldn't hear, anyhow." We were touched.

The flowers have an extraordinary brilliance there. Such pansies! And the columbine! that is the most splendid of all. Almost everyone has it — great double blossoms, almost as large as tiger lilies, of all the colors of earth, ranging from dark blue to bright yellow, lavender, pink. We stopped beside someone's garden, where a man was down on his hands and knees weeding a flower-bed. We spoke to him in a friendly way about his garden. Immediately he got up and picked us a great bunch of the exquisite columbine, with some pansies. It seems as if the Nova Scotians make the very best of their short summers, cramming into their gardens every flower that can possibly find an inch of soil to fasten its roots in.

* * *

THE next day, Sunday, we went down to say good-bye to those of the *Norman D*. In our forgetfulness, we never thought about its being Sunday until, as we drew very near the schooner and were walking along on the railroad tracks, we met the crew face to face. We stepped back amazed. Bill, Bob, Roy, and Irish Bill, all marching along in a body, all with new dark blue suits, all with newly shined shoes, all in clean white shirts and ties! Every atom of their charm, their character, had vanished out of them. Before, they were sailors. Now they were nothing — nothing at all. Even the mate was considerably less piratical and delightful.

It threatened rain, and the mate said he had decided not to go ashore at all, but to return to the schooner with us. "I don't want to get my clothes wet," said he. Care-free Mate Bill worrying about getting his clothes wet! But the other three were determined to go on to town to "show off." We left them, and went to the schooner with the mate. Even the steward was slightly dressed up. He had on a clean apron, or a clean blue cotton shirt, or another pair of trousers; he looked different, somehow. The captain was dressed up like a young boy; and he looked like a monkey, a positive monkey, in his shore clothes.

It began to rain hard and furiously. We had just time to duck into the cabin. The three of the crew who had persisted in heading towards town came running back at full speed and leaped over the side of the schooner. We had quite a party down there. The mate took our blankets and rolled them into a beautiful roll, marline-hitching them with stout cord, and tying them as only a sailor could. Even a professional mountain-climber could do no better. Then I went with him in to his bunk, and we had a farewell talk. There was a snapshot on the wall of his little room — a snapshot of a girl. The mate indicated it, saying to me:

"You know, my wife, she's awful funny, and she sends me all sorts o' things, just to tease me. She sent me that picture while we was down there in New Haven."

"Who is she?"

"Oh, she's a girl I used to go with. I went with her three years. Yes, I had pretty strong intentions of hookin' up with that girl!"

"What happened that you didn't?"

"Well, I met t' other one. Her father had died, 'n' she was livin' there all alone, 'n' so I went to her instead."

"Have you seen the other girl since?"

"Yes, a few times. She give me the dickens fer goin' to the other, 'n' that was all there was to it." Then he talked about his career. He gave a sigh and said: "If I had my hull life t' live over, I'd do it powerful diff'rent — that is, if I knowed as much as I know now."

"Would you go to sea, mate?"

"Not if I knowed as much as I know now."

"What do you think you would do?"

"Well, I reckon I'd 'a' been a barber. That's a very pleasant little job. But bein' a sailor is good in some ways. I keep thinkin' I'm goin't' resign at th' next port, but somethin' about it — I dunno, but I seem t' stick. It's a good, healthy life, out in the open, 'n' that's somethin'."

* * *

WE went back to our hotel for supper, with an agreement that the mate was to run up that way later, when he went ashore, and that we should be on the lookout for him about six o'clock. The captain was to come up, too, to write that note which he had promised so long ago — a note for identification, stating that we were his passengers on the schooner, to be handed to any officials who might challenge us in Boston. We were sitting in the hotel, talking, about six o'clock, and watching for Bill. Sure enough, we saw him striding along, in company with Irish Bill. As for the skipper, we didn't see him. But the two Bills went straight on, appearing not even to see the place. I darted out the door like a flash and called out "Hi! Mate!" in a loud and hearty voice. Several persons turned at the sound of that "Mate!"

I asked him why he hadn't stopped. He said he thought it was much too grand a place for the likes of him (he was in his half-sailor, half-shore clothes, which were at least better than his real shore clothes). I said that was nonsense, and asked him if he didn't want to come in. He agreed briefly, though still feeling a little shy, and Irish Bill went on walking up the street, alone.

"Where's Bill going?" I asked.

"I dunno. Bill's a queer lad, he is."

Then my shipmate appeared, and the three of us set out for a walk together. We were discussing the old man and wondering where he was, when suddenly we met him face to face. "I've just been up-town for a little walk," said he. We turned and went back toward the hotel. My shipmate was extremely eager not to let the old man slip between his fingers and once more dodge writing that note. We went in, and I sat with Mate Bill while the old man wrote it. I saw him throw it away at least twice as if dissatisfied.

As for Mate Bill and me, our talk ran on to the jackknife which I had promised him.

"I'll send it up to Bridgewater as soon as I get home, mate," said I.

"That will be fine, Barbara," said he. "I'll be awful glad to have it. But listen, don't send it to my home *address*, will you?" (He had given me his home address before.) "Be sure not to send it there, Barbara," he went on, very earnestly, "Because, you see, my wife'd get the package, 'n' she'd open it, 'n' w'at would she find but a jackknife? 'N' from 'Barbara'! She wouldn't rillize that you was jist a little shipmate o' mine. She'd think you was a girl that I'd been goin' with, 'n' she'd be jealous, she would. I know how it is, 'cause I got in trouble with her that way once before. I'd get in wrong with her, you see, 'n' I wouldn't like to have that. So don't, will you, Barbara?"

"No, I promise you I won't, mate," said I, in the same earnest tone. "I'll send it right up to Bridgewater, and as soon as I get home, too, so that it'll get up here to you before the schooner sails." The rest of our conversation was on the same theme — warning me against sending the knife to his home address — until the end, when a strange thing happened.

"Was your mother worried 'bout havin' you come on the schooner?" said Bill.

"No! Why should she be?"

"Well, I thought, perhaps, you bein' the on'y woman aboard, she might git worried. But she didn't need to, anyhow. I know one that wouldn't let you be imposed upon — and that one is — *me!*"

By this time the captain had finished, and it was just when they were going out the door that Bill said: "Good-bye, shipmate!" and I replied: "Goodbye, shipmate!"

And that was the last I saw of Bill.

* * *

AS for the captain's note, it ran like this:

June 25th/27

> This is to certify that
> Miss Barbara Follett and
> Mr. Bryn were my guests
> on board the sch Norman
> D from New Haven conn
> to Bridgewater N S and are
> returning home via the
> Yarmouth boat to Boston
> C. Avery Master
> Schn. Norman D

But it wasn't the Yarmouth boat that we took: it was the train. The next morning early, we started off by train and rode until we came to Digby. From Digby we took a little steamer across the Bay of Fundy to St. John, New Brunswick. For about three hours of the afternoon we steamed across the great bay. But there was no crew to talk to, no rigging. I couldn't have steered had I asked. Nothing was familiar. The wind blew my skirts so that I could hardly take a step — for there was a violent sailing breeze, though nothing like our gale. I wish we could have gone across in the schooner, before a whitecapped sea like this. It was glorious, except for the steadiness of the little ship, and the stiffness and unfamiliarity of it. The exit to Digby Harbor was heavenly — even lovelier than Lahave, if that were possible. It was very much bigger, and just as you thought you had the open sea ahead of you, you saw two great green arms of land — something like those at Lahave, but longer and slenderer and even more like arms — reaching out from the mainland and all but meeting.

We steamed out between those two long arms, through the narrow opening. For a long time afterward we could look back and back at the green against the vivid sky; then we were out of sight of land, and alone in the sea. We passed one little fisherman very much like the one which we had seen on the fifth day of the voyage in the schooner — the day the sailing breeze had just begun to come. I was delighted to see a sailing vessel again. Almost as soon as we were out of sight of Digby we came in sight of the hills and mountains in back of St. John — billowing dark blue hills, reaching up and up above the horizon; and at last we saw the city itself. A few minutes later the steamer chugged into St. John, and we disembarked.

There isn't anything to say about the place. My mind was dwelling wholly on the voyage just past; everything else was unimportant. We took the train from there, staying on it all night, and in the morning arrived in Boston. From Boston we took the train to New Haven, and arrived there four hours later. The only interesting thing that happened in the whole train ride was that, passing over the border between New Brunswick and Maine, the custom-house official strode through the train asking for identifications. He was very pleasant about it.

I showed Captain Avery's amusing little note, and Mr. Holbrook's affidavit, useful at last.

Mother was to meet us at New Haven. We came walking up through the station with our luggage — including the roll of blankets tied by Bill, which had stayed faithfully tied through thick and thin on the train. Mother said afterward that she could see nothing but my glowing scarlet face and two rows of great white teeth as I grinned. Sun, wind, and salt sea had left their mark upon me!

Everything I had once anticipated and dreamed of took place. I found myself twice as strong and hearty as before. I swanked, and I still rolled just a little, though that had pretty well worn off by this time. I told my stories, in a gay manner and in a hearty sailor voice, all the way home and for days afterward — all as I had often planned.

When I ran up the steps at home, the first person I saw was

my friend Mr. Rasmussen. I ran to him at once with huge sailor leaps, and said, shaking him warmly by the hand: "Thanks, Mr. Rasmussen, for sending me to Nova Scotia! Weather? We had thick fog and calm most of the time — but one good, ripping northeast gale."

"Well, you sure look husky enough to have been a sailor. Thick fog 'n' calm, did you have? And nor'east wind? Hm! I kinda reckoned that was what you was getting."

* * *

THE next afternoon I kept my promise to Mate Bill by going in town to buy him a bully stout jackknife. I wrote him a shipmate-ish letter at the same time, asking him, among other things, to keep a lookout for a poncho and some other things which I had managed to leave on the schooner. I received a letter from him shortly in answer. I wrote to him again, and received another letter. But when I wrote a third time, asking him to keep on writing to me, because I didn't want to lose track of him, and because I *did* want to sail with him again sometime, I got no answer; nor have I heard from him since. But here, hoping you will not ridicule them in spite of their imperfections, are his letters. It is delightful to me to have them — the evidence that I have at last made acquaintance with a true sailor. The first is as follows:

The Voyage of the Norman D.

Bridgewater
July 4 1929

Well shipmate
I recived your letter was glad to hear that you rive bame saft again well Barbara your things you was speaking about they are here the old man sed he would send them to you From new york
we leave here July 5 for new york. I will soon be hearing the sail flap again The old man is no better the steward and him still talk fit some times But I gest it will be talk I would like to see you here to go Back with us

Barbara Newhall Follett

> *I no you like to go to sea*
> *what king of a trip did you*
> *have gone home*
> *so long from your shipmate*
> *Bell*

And here is the second:

> New york
> July
> th 30 1927

well Barbara
I reicived the jack-knife
sent I came in hear I had left Bridgewater
befor the knife reach there so they sent it
to me here
so now I am trying to think how I am
gone to return the gif
we was 16 days comming over hear we had fight
fog all the way over and lots of head wind
I thought we was never gone to get here

The Voyage of the Norman D.

Barbara I am sending your things to you I
spoke to the old man about them and he
made no after to send then so I thought
I would send them to you
I hop you get them all right
we will be here about a week longer yet for we
leave I don't no where we are gone from hear yet
well So long Barbara from your shipmate
W H m

There they are. W. H. M. is William Henry McLeod. There is my shipmate. I've told you all about him that I know — and all that I know about the trip.

And so, Alan, with hearty, piratical good wishes for the best of luck — good-bye!

Your shipmate

Blackheart

Afterword
Stefan Cooke

BARBARA NEWHALL FOLLETT (1914-1939?), the twelve-year-old girl whose first book, *The House Without Windows*, had received glowing reviews in the United States and Europe, was not one to bask in glory nor rest for long. The same month that Alfred A. Knopf published her book, Barbara wrote a long letter to one of her favorite correspondents, Edward Porter St. John (1866-1953). It mentions her latest piece of writing — *Poppy Island*, a "pirate song" — and describes the idea behind her next story, which would also feature pirates.

First, here's beautiful, haunted *Poppy Island*:

> — I —
> There are hundreds of isles among the seas,
> And scores where pirates used to go;
> But only one in the whole wide world
> Where flaming scarlet poppies grow.
>
> Like emerald glowing in azure and pearl,
> With winding flowery patterns of gold,

Stefan Cooke

Lies Poppy Island; and even the gulls
Muffle their wings, and cry "Behold!"

With crystal shells the sand is pearled—
Foam-fringed sand, white and gleaming—
Cliffs dip down into azure and green—
Gull-haunted crags, towering, dreaming.

Like falling trees in a mountain-storm
Are the waves that topple and madly race
The spray is high, the sea is snowing
And edging the beaches in delicate lace.

The vivid, butterfly-luring green
Quivers and rustles; the tropic isle
Spreads its arms to the smiling sky.
And on their hill the poppies smile.

—II—
Dazzling, sunburned treasure lies buried,
Sleeping, bright as sun on the sea;
Sleeping within a strong sea-chest
Locked with a jewel-encrusted key.

It lies there sleeping—sleeping, dreaming—
Dreaming of pirates who left it there,
Dreaming of sinister lovers of gold,
Each of them risking his life for a share.

It is buried high on a shadowy hill.
Amid the sombre green and brown
There burns a banner of flaunting red
To guard the place where treasure went down—

Afterword

The brilliant red of waving poppies,
Flowers to guard the pirate gold.
Strange, how strange! but this is the tale
Of flowers, pirates, and treasure they told.

—III—
As a garden-box, the old sea-chest
Rested once on a moss-smooth lawn—
The lawn of a garden glowing with sunset
Of tulips, and poppies the colour of dawn.

But Blackbeard raided the sea-girt town.
His pirates must sail with no delay;
And, richly laden with sparkling bangles,
They spilled the flowers, and sped away.

To sea, to sea! and the old chest too—
Where ships talk softly, alone with the sky;
But poppy-seeds clustered between the bands
Of the iron-bound chest—and they did not die.

Blackbeard's gold! The heart of that man
Was darker than all his treasure was bright.
The great chest filled and filled with wealth
From many a raid and many a fight.

—IV—
Such treasure a pirate had never beheld—
All taken under the Skull and Bones,
From many a gallant and goodly ship
Sent calling untimely on Davy Jones—

Lustrous rubies, odd ingots of gold,

Stefan Cooke

Diamonds, garnets shining like blood,
Silver in waterfalls snowy with foam,
Pieces of eight, like rivers in flood.

But the coins of gold! oh, the coins of gold
In dazzling, blinding fire-cascades!
Dubloons, guineas, moidores, and more,
Like the island sun that never fades;

And more, and more, unbroken streams—
Lakes, and seas, and mountains of gold;
The wealth of the pirates that sailed the sea
Is a fairy-tale, to be left untold.

But strangest of all their hard-won gems
Were trinkets of delicate metal lace—
Fillets encrusted with opals and pearls
That once surmounted some fair maid's face;

Bangles of pearl like fairy foam,
Curious bracelets of golden spray,
Adornments like feathery mountain-frost
Decking the wings of a dancing fay.

—V—
The chest was full. Blackbeard arose:
"Now bullies, come, we must hide our duff
Where none but ourselves will ever go;
Then beat up for more—aye, that's the stuff!

"Be sure to put no hands ashore —
By the powers, I'll not be cheated again.
Mutiny follows, and all ill-luck,

Afterword

For putting treasure ashore with men.

*"The last time, we marooned a man:
And, swollen with revengeful pride,
He moved the treasure and covered it well,
And gleefully then lay down and died.*

*"Take care, take care, lest this happen again."
He gave five pieces of gold to each;
They lowered the boat, and muffled their oars,
And landed the chest on the island beach.*

*Then through the vivid tropic glades,
Over dank moss, to the shadowy hill—
Murmuring grimly, with cutlasses drawn:
"Him who bothers this, him we will kill!"*

*By a ferny palm they buried it deep,
And spaded and tumbled the thick clods on—
But how should they know of those other gems,
The deathless seeds of the flower of dawn?*

*Then Blackbeard plotted his secret map,
In vivid green, with the tree in red.
Long before night, with his pirate band,
Away from that mystic place he sped.*

—VI—
*But the seeds were there, in twinkling clusters;
And how those tiny specks of gold
Valiantly pushed the earth away,
Thrusting up through the leafy mold!*

Stefan Cooke

*Up they lifted their pale green shoots
To the quivering sun of the southern skies,
And wondered to see the gaudy wings
Of blazing tropic butterflies.*

*One scarlet blossom trembled there—
Another — others; each fragile stem
Was crowned with its shallow cup of fire,
And the hilltop grew alight with them.*

*Like a crimson dew the petals fall,
Seeds shower down like golden rain;
And seasons pass. But where are those
Who should come and find their gold again?*

*—VII—
Ah, where indeed? Beneath the waves
Among the dead who tell no tales;
And nevermore need the Seven Seas
Beware of them and their blood-stained sails.*

*But the poppies remember Blackbeard's men:
The fire above guards the fire below,
And flies their color, the color of blood.
Do they rest in peace, remembered so?*

*Their treasure is flaunted and betrayed!
To the far horizon it stands revealed!
Can they lie still in their watery graves,
With their richest hoard to men's eyes unsealed?*

*—VIII—
Now we will wait, and watch, and see,*

Afterword

Behind thick shrubs on the shadowy hill;
Ghosts of those pirates are filing along:
"Him who bothers this, him we will kill!"

Robed in the garments in which they died,
Eyes still cruel, faces still brown,
Each has a cutlass clenched in his teeth,
To defend the place where treasure went down.

Blackbeard still is in the lead.
His tunic, as in days of old,
Is bound with ghosts of amethysts
Set deep in reddest burning gold.

They look as once they looked in life,
But make not even the ghost of a sound.
They gather about the old, frayed map;
And now the treasure-place is found.

But when they see the poppies there,
They huddle together in deadly fear;
They eye each other, as terrified
As if the King of Hell were near.

Shivering slightly, Blackbeard turns,
And speaks in a dreadful, ghostly tone:
" 'Tis an evil omen, my bullies; come
Away from there, and leave it alone."

—IX—

The dew is falling, deep, soft pearls;
Dusk swoops down on the vivid isle;
Only the poppies stay, undimmed—

Only the poppies quietly smile.

One by one, the pirate ghosts
Vanish now in the budding dark
And, slipping through the blackened woods,
Sail away in their ghostly barque.

I have told my tale of the Poppy Island,
Haunted by gulls that echo the cries
Of "Gold!" and "Blood!" that once went
    sounding
Shrilly through those windy skies.

And here's an excerpt from that January 1927 letter to Mr. St. John, in which Barbara explains the idea behind her pirate story:

> But besides this pirate song, I have managed to find time for a story. To be sure, it isn't written yet, but I have such a firm idea of what I mean to write that it will be very little trouble when I once get buckled down to it. It is about a little girl (nothing like Eepersip, however) who was always having strange, fantastic ideas about things, but most especially about pirates and gypsies. She writes little odd, quaint stories about everything she sees, and wants to be a gypsy herself. When her family moves from a tiny country village to a large city, she begins the business of fortune-telling, with the aid of a friend of hers — and for beautiful, written fortunes she is given various little odds and ends, mostly trinkets; and in this way she collects the necessities for a gypsy costume, until, finally, she is able to wander about dressed just like a gypsy — with golden bangles, and pearl bangles, and bracelets, and anklets, and a full flouncy skirt

Afterword

with bright embroideries. But it is her ideas and her writings that will make the main part of this *biography*; for I expect to put in many of them just as she might have written them. And in these stories, though she loved things of Nature, and was constantly making butterflies and birds and flowers play the main parts in her stories — she wrote mostly about pirates and gypsies; for her idea of pirates was much the same, mystic, blood-and-gold, unknown-isle as mine; and her idea of gypsies was simply a mysterious tribe who wore the golden bangles she was so fond of, and who told fortunes — just as she did. I am so overflowing with ideas for this new story that — well, if this letter should suddenly break off in the midst of a line or sentence, you would know why; I would be simply overwhelmed with a flood of irresistible ideas.

Despite these irresistible ideas, there's no evidence in the Follett archives at Columbia University that Barbara began such a pirate story. Of course, early 1927 was a particularly busy time following the publication of *The House Without Windows*. On top of the regular schoolwork and music lessons assigned by her mother, Helen (1883-1970), there were interviews with the press, at least one live broadcast on the radio, and many letters that required attention. There was also the matter of experience. How could Barbara write about pirates when she hadn't set foot on a vessel larger than a rowboat? Reading about pirates and the sea would not suffice; she would simply have to find a ship to sail on and earn her sea legs.

Before we get to the *Norman D.*, however, it's important to know about the crisis brewing within the Follett family — a crisis that weighed mighty heavily on Barbara's mind. Her father, Wilson (1887-1963), whom she loved dearly, had been staying away from home for increasingly long periods of time.

At first he maintained that his heavy workload as editor for Knopf in New York was the reason, but Helen and Barbara were not convinced. Barbara expressed her dismay in a letter on April 29, 1927:

> Dear Daddy: It seems to us that New York must be a sort of Louis XI's palace full of snares, temptations, pit-falls, traps, and everything else for enticing and entangling its helpless victims.

Helen's and Barbara's suspicions proved correct. I think that Wilson (who was my grandfather) had already become entangled in an affair with my grandmother, Margaret Whipple (1906-1995), a fellow Knopf employee who wasn't much older than Barbara herself. Wilson would abandon Helen, Barbara, and Sabra, his youngest daughter, for good around Barbara's fourteenth birthday, in March 1928.

In intimate letters to Anne-White Meservey, an old family friend who stood by the deserted Folletts, Helen described just how much Barbara had worshipped and depended on her father. Not only was he the girl's literary mentor, he had been Barbara's eager companion on the wilderness adventures they enjoyed so much. Wilderness and adventure were Barbara's two greatest loves in life. These excursions, which took place near the cottage the family rented on Little Lake Sunapee, New Hampshire, began when Barbara was ten. In late September 1924, she and Wilson spent a week camping and canoeing the Ossipee and Chocorua Lakes before climbing Mount Chocorua, Barbara's first summit of that fine mountain. The following October they spent several days in a cabin on top of Mt. Moosilauke, surrounded by swirling wintery mist and hoar frost — the "frost feathers" that delighted Barbara so, as you'll see in the description below. And in the fall of 1926 they

Afterword

climbed up cascading Flume Brook in Franconia Notch — much of it after dark with Wilson carrying a too-heavy pack and a failing flashlight — to a campsite on Mount Liberty. They camped several nights and explored the ridges and summits of the Franconia Range. It was Barbara's last adventure with her father.

Frost Feathers — seen October, 1925 and 1926

Frost feathers are not, as is commonly supposed, the delicate traceries and "paintings" of Jack Frost found on window-panes. Indeed, they are not a consequence of frost at all. They are found at high altitudes, after a cold windy night and very thick mist.

They are frozen mist — mist which freezes onto the rocks when it touches them — built up and chiseled away from the wind — chiseled until they have scalloped or crinkled edges, and until they are in the shape of a feather more perfect and lovely than any bird-feather — a feather, which, when taken apart, is found to consist of thin brittle layers. Each one has an individual tracery and pattern of its own — delicately shown in the snow-white.

Sometimes they are seen hanging almost in a semi-circle, off crags; sometimes striking out into the wind, sometimes, when on the lee side of things, rounder, like small inner bird-feathers, and lying close to the rocks, scalily; sometimes they form on the exposed tips of trees, and sometimes so thickly that the small limbs are glossy and rounded with them, like a white cat's tail; once we found them in exquisite little rosettes around the wire cables which anchor the Moosilauke Top House; we found them around the grindstone; often we saw exquisite caves of them, pointing every which way as the wind had swirled about; on Haystack we saw them on the tall, skinny, gnarled trunks of burnt trees, making them seem like pointing or beckoning mountain-ghosts; again they are seen, delicately rippled on the very ground — we found them formed over cranberry beds, where the juice of the frozen berries had pinkened all the snow — there the frost feathers had all their exquisite fairy-like traceries all in a sublime pink.

The largest ones form in giant clusters — two-foot ones, down to one-inch ones, all joining together from the same root or clump, and peering out boldly into the cool pearliness of mist, and the wind-sculptor.

We seemed to be in fairyland when we wandered on the Knife-edge through paradises of them.

LET'S RETURN to Barbara's interest in pirates, which would soon evolve into a love for sailing ships and the sea. Pirates surfaced early in Barbara's life through books, and who better than her well-read parents and their literary friends to recommend stories that would spark her imagination and desire to read and learn more? Without a doubt she devoured *Peter and Wendy* and *Treasure Island* several times each, not to mention memoirs such as Richard Henry Dana Jr.'s *Two Years Before the Mast*. But it was her friendships with two men in particular that enflamed her love of pirates and the sailing ships of old. Both men are integral to *The Voyage of the Norman D*.

The first of these was Leo Anthony Meyette (1894-1974), a farmer's son and sometime grocery clerk in Georges Mills, near Little Lake Sunapee. Leo had befriended the Folletts in 1922 or earlier; I think earlier is likely since he was living in New Haven in 1917, and the record shows that he and Wilson had hiked together in New Hampshire when Barbara was too young to tag along. Barbara nicknamed Leo "Alan" — the same

Afterword

Alan to whom the long letter that is *The Voyage of the Norman D.* was addressed — while she called herself "Blackheart." Like Barbara, Leo was a keen explorer of the mountains and forests near Barbara's "Cottage in the Woods." To Barbara's sorrow, however, she watched him sail away from New York on the *Leviathan* late in 1924; and that was by no means his last journey from home. In 1927 he sailed to the Philippines where he would serve as headmaster of a school for Moro children in Indanan on the island of Jolo, and so letters crossing the ocean would have to make do.

Leo wrote to Barbara on the fourth day of his voyage aboard the United States Army Transport ship *Thomas*, on June 14, 1927. In fact, Barbara's reply to this letter became *The Voyage of the Norman D.*

> Dear Blackheart:
>
> This could never be a pirate ship for the reason that there are five congressmen and their wives and families on board to say nothing of about one hundred army officers and their wives and families who are on their way to Guam or Manila. I cannot imagine anything piratical or romantic about this crowd. I did see a very desperate looking sailor walking the deck. I am sure that he had several knives concealed about his person and I am in hopes that there is a mutiny brewing. Everything is almost too calm and serene to last. So I have hopes.
>
> Coming thru Nevada on the train I stopped at a little station and headed up to the platform were two rather desperate looking characters on horse back. The horses were rather fiery looking and the men wore large sombreros and good looking overalls. I hoped that they might be going to hold up the train but they must have changed their mind upon seeing such a desperate looking character as your Alan

for they drove off in an immense cloud of dust while we were still at the station. That was the nearest thing to any excitement on the way out.

San Francisco is like all cities but it has a very beautiful park only that it is laid out too much in squares and rectangles of flower beds. In it I saw the most magnificent bear. He seemed as tall and broad as our horse Maggie. His paws must have been almost a foot wide and nearly a foot and a half long. He certainly was immense. I enjoyed seeing him stamp around his yard and wished that I might be able to let him loose to see what he would do.

By the way coming out I saw some very rugged snow capped mountains that made my feet itch to get off the train and start for the very top of them.

Last night we had a very beautiful sunset and the afterglow thru the clouds reminded me very much of the view looking southeast from the top of Moosilauke on a semi clear morning when the clouds open and shut. It was very nice. I managed to get where there were not many people and had a very pleasant half hour watching it.

We are getting into the tropics now and the weather is much warmer. I confess that I am enjoying it. I was very cold in San Francisco and it took me several days to get warm again. Friday we were due to arrive at Honolulu and I understand that we stay there two days. I will write you of anything interesting that I may see. Then on to Guam and then Manila where we are due to arrive on the fifth or sixth of July. I imagine that I will be rather fed up with the boat and its passengers but as I see no possibility of getting off I will make the best of it.

Please let me know, if you know where there is any treasure buried in this part of the world and I will go after it at any cost on a fifty-fifty basis.

Afterword

To the last dubloon,
Alan
My best to all of the family.

Eighteen years later Helen would write a book, *Men of the Sulu Sea* (Charles Scribner's Sons, New York, 1945), about Leo Meyette's remarkable achievements at the Moro school. Not only did he teach the children English, he introduced many crops and farming techniques to the locals, built wood and machine shops, brought the first rice mill to the island, formed and led a Boy Scout troop, oversaw the printing of the school newspaper, and, in 1937, helped rebuild the entire campus after a typhoon ravaged the island. There are many more examples of Leo's accomplishments in Helen's book. Leo represented his country very well, as Helen emphasized on page 65:

> No visitor ever forgot the headmaster, a Yankee from New Hampshire. He satisfied so completely the idea of the right American in the right place. Here was a man who found himself as much at home on a Sulu island among Moslem boys as on a New England farm among the village schoolboys — a rugged six-footer, heavily built, with character and strength in his face, kindness and humor in his dark eyes.
>
> Always he inspired respect and confidence, as you could see. And it wasn't surprising that, unlike other Americans before him, he never carried a gun for self-protection, and that he removed the iron bars from the windows of his house because he'd be hanged if he wouldn't rather take a chance on having his head lopped off by some crazed Moro, than live behind bars. Still, there was something about him, perhaps that keen look in his eyes, that said he was a good shot if shooting had to be done, a look that sons of pirates and reformed pirates themselves didn't fail to recognize.

A new type of New England schoolmaster? Perhaps, rather, he was a combination of the old-fashioned and the modern. He had arrived at Jolo one day, some years back, on a Chinese junk, and had brought with him, among other things, a pack full of homespun philosophy, flavored with humor and enriched with commonsense ideas, a confidence in his ability to work with people wherever he found them, and to work with his own hands, and, above all, the cheerful belief that schoolboys were the same the world over.

Yes, the Moro children were the sons and grandsons of true pirates! Barbara would have loved to visit them and Leo — I have no doubt. In 1928, however, Leo wrote that he was engaged to be married and — not surprisingly since her father had just abandoned his own family — Barbara was adamant that Leo reverse course.

July 10, 1928

Hail, mate Alan!

And yet, on second thoughts, not "hail" neither, but "get to the devil." That was what I meant to say. Alan, Alan, shame on you! Alan, if you knew how I felt, walking home from New London yesterday afternoon, as I read those cursed words of your letter — Alan, if you knew how I felt then, you would turn into salt water. Why, Alan, you've gone to work and taken malicious joy in busting three perfectly good hearts already — your own sister's, mine, and Helen's. If not even the cat's. For I am sure she feels it, too.

Alan, you must not marry. You must not. I am going to talk to you and damn you up and down to the devil like a Dutch uncle, so be prepared. Alan, Alan, you must not marry. Do you hear me? Oh, hell — would you could hear

Afterword

my voice, with the true quiver of rage and sorrow in it, instead of reading these dull written words. If I had a red ribbon I would write with that — it would be more the color of hell.

Alan, you must not marry. Do you understand me? Can you hear me, across these mad seas? Shipmate, shipmate, I am not trying to be unkind; don't you see I am only trying to save you? Alan, you would be the sickest and saddest and sorriest pirate on all the seven seas, if you allowed that moment of weakness to conquer you. Alan, if you marry, I'm done with you — you've lost one of the best friends you ever had. You didn't know I was one of your best friends, did you? But I am.

Alan, I can't have this. I am hurt to the very heart already; and if you go and do it, I don't see how I can bear it. Don't you remember anything at all? Didn't you practically swear to stay free and wild and happy? Oh, when I think of it all! It is too terrible. Do you remember when you were shingling the roof of the farm, and the urge for climbing a mountain came suddenly over you, and you threw your hammer into the air and climbed a mountain? You mean to tell me you don't remember when you were making a door, and felt that same mad impulse, and left the house chock-full of chips, sawdust, and shavings? Oh, Alan, Alan, Alan! How can I support this? Tell me, shipmate, how am I to support it? Have you thought at all? Have you thought how sorry you yourself will be?

Alan, I should have been far less surprised to see the sun collide with the moon and throw off a tremendous shower of brilliant sparks, which fell to the earth and turned into opals bigger than grape-fruits — far less surprised to see this than to see Alan Gold-belt getting married. It is, with absolutely no exception, the very last of the possible or impossible that I expected. Absotively and posolutely, the very last. And also the very last that I should have liked to see.

Do you remember the time we were out walking, Alan, and you suddenly said: "Bar, can you imagine me in any other way than ragged, penniless, and out of a job? Could you imagine me married?" And I said I certainly could not. And I can not. I mercifully can hardly believe my senses. For if I could believe them, I think I should sink into the earth.

You must not, you must not, YOU MUST NOT! Don't you understand, mad shipmate? Where's your freedom now, where will it be later? Where the mad adventures, where the rivers of gore and mountains of rotting flesh? Leo, we won't look at you with a wife. If you have her, keep away from us, that's all, or we'll blow you up and send you to your lover, the devil who resides in the land known as Hell. You keep away from us, and we'll keep away from you, for, by thunder, we'll not be shipmates any more, you and I, Alan. You're no true pirate. You're a disgrace to the ship, and must walk the plank, or swing from the yard-arm.

I boil with rage. Alan, Alan, Alan, who used to be my shipmate, my pirate friend, my treasure-hunting companion — how can you go and bust up my heart into little hard splinters like that. Need I remind you of the grocery days, when you sent high-hatters astray so maliciously and gloriously? Those persons whom you misdirected to Soonipi Park are undoubtedly driving away yet to the eastward. Need I remind you of the day we followed the gorgeous little brook in the winter, walking on mysterious snowy soap-bubbles which let us down into caves and chasms; of the time we hiked over the hills and valleys to Little Sunapee, and over some more hills and valleys home? Need I remind you of all that? Alan, do you hear me? Do you hear me?

Afterword

Well, I am hurt; and when I am hurt I am hard as nails, and bitter as the salt sea. I would save you, my shipmate, if I could, but the ultimate decision lies with you. You know my mind now. You must write to me, and tell me what you have done, and whether you have given her up or not. And if you have done what you should do, we will welcome you in true piratical fashion — if not, go to the devil! I say again, Alan, for I'll no more of ye.

Your enraged shipmate,
Blackheart

Barbara's letter didn't work. Leo married Maybelle Wells (1895-1995) in Manila, and in 1940 they were settled in Claremont, New Hampshire, with two daughters. At that time Leo was working 65 hours a week as a car salesman and would soon become the dealership's manager. Despite his marriage, he and Barbara remained friends.

BARBARA's second piratical friend was an older man — the historian, biographer, poet, and editor George Sands Bryan (1879-1943). Bryan is best remembered for his biographies of Sam Houston and Thomas Edison; or, more appealingly to Barbara, for *The Camper's Own Book for Devotees of Tent and Trail*. In 1925 — perhaps on the recommendation of their friends the Folletts — George Bryan and his wife, Alice, vacationed on the north side of Little Lake Sunapee, across from the Cottage in the Woods that the Folletts rented from the Stanley family each summer. Wilson didn't accompany his family to Sunapee in 1925, but in a letter to Barbara he reminded her to paddle over to the Bryans' for violin practice. By that time she had renamed George "Captain Hook"; Alice Hook's right-hand man, "Smee"; and herself "Peter." The dedication in *The House Without Windows* is "for my two playmates J. H. and S. W. F." — that is, James Hook and Sabra Wyman Follett. (The first dedicatee is certainly not "F. H." as carelessly transcribed in later editions.)

George Bryan was intrigued by his young friend's insatiability for knowledge and beguiled by her enthusiasm for mystery and adventure. He was a willing companion in her quests for treasure hidden among the rocks and trees of Little Lake Sunapee. They would pass each other cryptic maps and notes in secret code.

When apart, George proved to be a witty, faithful correspondent and also a source of refuge when Barbara returned, devastated, from a trip to New York in early June 1928. She had taken the train down to the city to persuade her father to come home. Wilson shunned his daughter on his Perry Street doorstep, having convinced himself that it was better for his family, especially the worshipful Barbara, to sever all ties to him, give him a divorce, and allow him to remarry. The reasoning behind Wilson's demand was mainly financial: neither he, nor Helen, nor Margaret had any savings to live on, and the two Knopf paychecks were in jeopardy. In the 1920s a married man living with his mistress was a recipe for scandal, particularly when the man worked for a company as respectable as Knopf's. Indeed, Wilson and Margaret left the publishing house in July 1928. Willa Cather, a Knopf author, was not displeased, writing to Alfred Knopf on August 28th: "I surely don't lament Wilson Follett's departure. Prince Hamlets are awfully trying in business relations." Wilson promised to support his family when there was money to send, but to Helen's immense unhappiness no money ever came.

Afterword

A coded message from George Bryan, which Barbara solved in pencil.

The day after Barbara returned from Perry Street, utterly crushed, she took an early train to the Bryans' house in Pelham, New York, where she remained for at least a week. It was the first but not the last time that Barbara would run away from home. She had not warned her mother about the predawn journey.

So it's not a surprise that Barbara wanted George Bryan to be "shipmate" on her schooner trip to Nova Scotia in June 1927, and with Leo Meyette far away he was the obvious choice of her parents, too. Obtaining the permission of the captain and taking along a chaperone were the two requirements for her to go at all. Barbara might have preferred that her father sail with her, but my guess is that he was too preoccupied in New York, or that he was already removing himself from his daughter's orbit.

* * *

ON NOVEMBER 18, 1927, Blanche Knopf wrote to Barbara saying that Knopf would be delighted to publish her long letter to "Alan"; not surprising since *The House Without Windows* had garnered much attention and thousands of sales. At that time Wilson was four months away from deserting his family and, as was the case with *The House Without Windows*, he edited the manuscript before the galley pages were set. I've compared Barbara's account with my grandfather's line-edited copy and noted some differences. Aside from tightening Barbara's prose to the letter's benefit (mainly by striking repetitive prose whose meaning was already clear); excising the occasional tidbit (for example, the question of how much passage fare Bryan should offer the captain); and redacting the sailors' saltier language (no *damn*s or *hell*s in sight, while *bust his goddamned jaw* has been reduced to *bust his blankety-blank jaw*), the chief difference between the two is the disguising of several names, as mentioned in Knopf's *Note by the Publisher*. I see no harm in updating the record now that all the players in it are dead, however. Captain Avery was in real life Captain Read; the Folletts' lawyer was named David Daggett, not Holbrook; the hapless crewman Richardson was named Dixon; Mate

Afterword

Bill's last name was McClelland, not McLeod. For some reason the fiery cook's real name — Oscar Follett, no relation to Barbara — was left unchanged. But what about the schooner herself? You'll have noticed that the true name of the ship, the *Frederick H.*, doesn't appear in *The Voyage of the Norman D.* at all.

Whiteway, a schooner about the same size and shape as the Frederick H.

In the book's early pages Barbara meets Mr. Rasmussen, an elderly sailor turned carpenter who's working at the house next door. You'll recall that it's Rasmussen who mentions that a lumber schooner from Nova Scotia, the *Frederick H.*, is in harbor. The *Frederick H.*, a 390-ton, 152-foot long three-masted schooner, painted white, was built in Kenneth Cochrane's shipyard in Fox River, Nova Scotia, in 1920. (As Barbara mentions early on in her letter, the *Frederick H.* was "cut down" from over 400 to 390 tons to avoid the cost of enlisting a "certified mate," who were in short supply.) It was the largest schooner Cochrane had built and although I have not found a good photograph of her, he designed the *Frederick H.* along the lines of the *Whiteway*, which was built the year before by W.R. Huntley & Son in nearby Parrsboro.

Given Knopf's requirement that the identities of the book's characters be disguised, a new name for the *Frederick H.* was also necessary. Who better to provide it than another of Barbara's friends, Yale University Press editor Norman Vaux Donaldson (1891-1964)? After teaching English at Dartmouth College and Brown University, Wilson had joined Yale University Press in 1919 and edited there for about three years before landing his best job yet, at Knopf. The Folletts befriended Norman and his wife, Hildegarde (1898-1948), around that time. Hildegarde, who had graduated from the Royal Conservatory of Music in Brussels, had been Barbara's violin teacher since at least 1923, and that same year the Donaldsons visited the Folletts on Little Lake Sunapee. During and after her father's desertion, Norman became increasingly important to Barbara as her confidant. She wrote the following letter to him after Wilson made a loud visit to the Cottage in the Woods, on July 7, 1928. (*Sternway* was Barbara's rowboat, which she and Wilson had jury-rigged with a cedar mast, boom, and sail. She was named *Sternway* for her tendency to sail backwards.)

> Dear Shipmate:
> I would have written sooner, except that I spend a good deal of my time Constructing Something. Exactly what it is I don't quite know yet; but it looks like a cross between a prairie schooner and a gravy boat, built from memory. It isn't intended to be either; but it looks rather like that. And I work on it rather ferociously, from four till eight in the morning; for I must get it finished before next week, for next week Mr. and Mrs. Third Factor [*the Bryans*] are supposed to

Afterword

arrive — which is fortunate, since the Financial Transactions are growing extremely limited.

This is a wunnerful place for pondering on the problem of the universe. When I want to ponder, I take *Sternway* out to the swimming raft, tie her (a bowline in the end of her painter), hop out, lie down on the raft, and go to it. I was there a whole hour one day, wondering about the universe, but I found that it was a rather Large Subject. It made my little, little brain crack-crack. But the phil. . . holds firm. SHE is more true and alive than ever; myself is much more worth-while, in spite of occasional external difficulties (family scenes, etc.); and as for the Third Factor — well, the Third Factor is about the same, so far as I can see. [*"phil" stands for philosophy; a little more on this later.*]

Anyhow, it's grand up here. Oh, Norman, I wish you could see *Sternway* sail! I had her out in a raging westerly gale o' wind, day before yesterday; and by jings!, Norman, I nearly sailed her under water! I shipped over the leeboards, and there was no tacking her — I had to wear her, and she changed like lightning, the little boom whizzed over like mad, and nearly carried us all under the salt sea. If there had been anyone with me, I should have been more careful; as it was I was very reckless, for I held the sheet until the leeward side was far too low in the water, and until the slender spruce mast bent nearly double, and I felt sure she would snap clean in two. Or perhaps three.

And yesterday I had her out in a raging westerly wind. I couldn't resist letting her run before it, just for the speed, but I found getting home was Quite a Different Matter. I might have gotten there, sooner or later, but Sabra was with me then, and she got impatient, so there was nothing to do (no Crustimoney Proseedcake) but furl up and row home — which I did.

Did you go down to the *Mina* to deliver my message? If you didn't, I shall be angry. It was so mean of me to run off like that without saying goodbye.

There have been Family Scenes. But only when WF was up, and they Had It, if ever there was a case. But I retired to the raft, and thought how external all those things were, and how unimportant, and how beautiful the lake was, and how huge the universe was, and what a fly-speck the Earth is (God must have to use a microscope), and what They were missing, squabbling away in the cottage, and how fortunate I was to be able to keep myself from being drawn into it — and numerous helpful thoughts of this kind.

Say, I thought you were going to write to me! Go down to the *Mina Nadeau*, and then tell me about it, you . . . . . . ! And, by the way, why don't you and Hildegarde come up some week-end? Jings, but wouldn't we have a sail? Say, my hearty, you don't know nothin' 'bout ships, without you've seed Sternway. She'll lay it over on any ship you've ever seed before. Jings, I never seed a ship like her; I never seed a ship carry on like she done 'n that gale 'o wind t'other day. Say, shipmatey, she was sailin' some twenty knots, I'll wager; she was goin' too fast t'heave out the log, 'twould 'a hauled me out o' the ship!

But really, seriously, it's beautiful up here, shipmate. There are two hills; the western one fairly low, and fringed with spruces on the top, and the rest of it pastured; the eastern one is a little higher, and is bald on top — it thrusts its crown of gold-brown into the full sunlight; over behind them, a little to the east, but showing on the west shoulder of the eastern hill, is Royal Arch, a high hill covered with a thick spruce forest, always looming darkly over the nearer, lighter hills. Then there is a valley between them — a valley of maples which turn most gloriously in the fall — a green

Afterword

valley which spreads up both the hills like a soft fringe. And square between the two hills, down on the lake, is the Pine Grove, dark against the background of maples. It is the most beautiful bit of woods in the whole world — you could sail the Seven Seas forever without seeing its like; it is mostly of yellow pines, with their long, dark, massive needles; here and there are white pines, more delicate and pale, but less glorious to look at; there are so many spruces away in the heart of it, and hemlocks along the water's edge, with here and there a white birch; and on this side, at the very tip, there is one curious little maple. This maple has been distorted by the thickness of the pines, until it is nothing but a tall, curving trunk, with a patch (square in shape) of leaves at its top. And in the fall, the lower half of that patch turns to bright scarlet, while the upper half is still bright green, giving a most weird effect.

And the hermit-thrushes! Norman, there is no sound of bird or man or wind or sail or wave, in all the universe, so beautiful as the hermit-thrush singing at dawn or at dusk, his throat lifted. He perches on the very highest twig of some grand old tree, and after every trill he looks about him alertly, on a perpetual lookout, like the lookout on the fo'c'sle deck who whistles to himself through his melancholy two hours. But the thrush's song may not be compared to the sailor's whistling! That is, the whistling may not be compared to the song.

Jings, but life is worth living —— ain't it? You ought to see Treasure Island — it's a real little green island at the corner of the lake — a glorious little uninhabited place. The Third Factor has a place 'way down at t'other end of the Twin Lake — I should guess 'twas about fifteen minutes brisk, hearty rowing — not so good as when T. F. was just across the lake. But the fifteen minutes hearty rowing will be good for my arms. They are already much tougher 'n afore, by carrying cargo to the place where the Something is being constructed. I will tell you, by the way, what this Something is, when I know!

Till then, Adieu! And write to me, you "Self-Conceited Fool!"

Your shipmate,

~~Peter.~~ Barbara.

P.S. I just noticed that I signed your letter "Peter." I was the most surprised person in this universe, I tell you! You know why, don't you? That is T. F.'s appellation for me; and I clean forgot that this letter was to you! Isn't that the most absurd thing?

B. N. F

Following the publication of the *Norman D.* — Wilson now living full-time in New York with Margaret — the New Haven Folletts felt stranded while Barbara's sea rage continued at gale force. Nothing on the mainland could stop her; she had to go to sea again. While tentative plans for short excursions on two other sailing ships, the *Albert F. Paul* and the *Annie C. Ross*, fell through, Barbara managed to persuade her mother that her latest and grandest scheme — to follow the Smithsonian Institution's *Carnegie* to Barbados and perhaps even to the South Pacific — was their best course. The *Carnegie,* a beautiful brigantine about the same size as the *Frederick H.*, was a scientific research vessel that had sailed 250,000 nautical miles over six cruises since 1909. Barbara and Helen would take their typewriters, and soon Barbara would sign a contract with *Harper's Monthly* to publish her observations.

One might be surprised that Helen would consider such a trip, particularly since it meant leaving Sabra behind with a guardian, but there was a major factor that motivated her deci-

Afterword

sion to go: lack of cash. Wilson had agreed to support his family to the tune of $500 a month, but only when he was earning that kind of money. Since April he had forwarded his Knopf paychecks to Helen while he and Margaret scraped by on the latter's meagre salary and Wilson's essays and stories (he was a frequent contributor to several publications). But Alfred and Blanche Knopf would not condone Wilson's and Margaret's affair and their employment was terminated. They left Knopf in late July, and Helen's income ceased. Both Wilson and Margaret were desperate to leave New York, which they hated, particularly during the hot summer months. They rented an old farmhouse in Tenant's Harbor, Maine, and began work on their novels — Margaret's *The Kirbys* (G.P. Putnam's Sons, New York, 1931) and Wilson's *No More Sea* (Henry Holt & Company, New York, 1933). This left Helen without any income at all; in fact she would not receive any support from Wilson despite many desperate pleas to him throughout the rest of 1928 and much of 1929. The cost of living in New Haven was high compared to the tropics; also Barbara and Helen would have a little cash to take with them — Barbara's royalties and the $500 advance from *Harper's* for her articles, although using that would be a last resort before any articles were published. There would be rental income from the New Haven house to support Sabra, and Wilson had said he would send money when he could. Sailing off on an adventure seemed a rosier prospect than living unhappily in a fatherless home.

In May 1928 Barbara and Helen visited the *Carnegie* in Washington D.C., where Captain James Ault and his crew were preparing for a three-year cruise. Being Barbara, she quickly befriended the captain and crew, and climbed the rigging "clear to her royal yard." A few days later the pair left New Haven again, this time to see the *Carnegie* sail away from Newport News, Virginia. Her first port of call was Plymouth,

England, followed by Hamburg, then Reykjavik, and at last she embarked on the long sail to Bridgetown, Barbados. Captain Ault planned to arrive there in early September.

Barbara aboard the Carnegie, 1928

Barbara wrote to Mr. Oberg, her longest-serving correspondent, describing the scene in Newport News: "This time we

Afterword

saw her off to England, under her sail, and I saw she was a beautiful thing to see, with that column of square canvas, one above the other, swaying and lifting and rolling against a bright sky — swaying over the big swells."

In keeping with his somewhat intractable nature, Wilson was firmly opposed to his wife leaving New Haven and Sabra behind for the tropics. He and Helen exchanged several long, antagonizing letters in the summer of 1928; these depict Wilson disagreeing with just about every suggestion Helen might make. He correctly foresaw that difficulties would arise between often-ill-tempered Helen and her semi-wild fourteen-year-old as they navigated uncharted waters for an indefinite length of time. On August 5 he warned his wife: "As a fact, I believe that there'll have to be a lot more iron in your control of her in the next two or three years, or else she'll go completely to pot." He also thought that Barbara wouldn't be able to produce installments for *Harper's* deemed good enough for publication. That also turned out to be true, although I think Barbara's writing about her experiences was always worth publishing, and the surviving pieces from the West Indies and South Pacific are no exception.

Understandably, Helen was ambivalent about the trip herself, but there were no particularly good options available following Wilson's desertion. Teaching school in Boston was a possibility, but Helen, who'd taught before Barbara was born, was far from keen on the idea. In reply to Wilson's letter of August 5, however, she offered an olive branch:

> Will you go to the West Indies and beyond with Barbara? It would be the greatest thing in the world for both of you. And all you will need is your passport, your typewriter, your passage; with Barbara's job, and the kind of stuff you can write, there isn't a chance in the world of your not working

your way along indefinitely. At Barbados you can pick up schooners; and the two of you can earn your way so much more easily than Bar and I can, for, as you know, I can never hope to earn money with my pen or typewriter. So far as Sabra and I are concerned, I have a standing invitation to teach in a school in Boston, and have Sabra with me. You wouldn't have to think of us at all, this I can promise you.

Won't you try it? You still have time to get a passport. And you would be free of New York, and you would get some health back, would have a gorgeous time with Bar, would be able to do many things with her that I cannot possibly do, would make the trip a far richer affair — and you would make me exceedingly happy.

Thanks so much for your kind and detailed letter, the advice of which I shall try to follow. I shall, however, have to go down, anyway, inasmuch as I can't have my wisdom tooth out by correspondence.

Unsurprisingly, the olive branch was rejected. Wilson wrote back on August 11:

As to going to the West Indies, I have no ideas except these: (1) My whole instinct and wish, the instant I can shed New York, will be to head north, not south; (2) I don't feel like heading anywhere leaving debts behind me — anywhere, that is, that would make a difference to my contact with the debts or to my rate of payment; and (3) I've responsibilities other than financial which wouldn't be at all well served by my running away with Barbara, and which I should still need to serve even if I didn't heartily want to, as I do. To thus much I might add that if by spectacular luck I should get abreast of the financial difficulties with any margin of ease to spare, I should want to use the margin to make something of

Afterword

myself after all these years, and to get out a few of the things that I've had seething where they make me uncomfortable. Barbados may be the way to accomplishment for you, but it isn't for me. I don't put myself first, but I don't see any good reason for not putting myself next after the discharge of my material obligations.

Wilson and Margaret drove north to Maine, while Barbara and Helen steamed south. On September 15 they boarded Lampert & Holt's steamship *Voltaire* in New York and sailed third class to Bridgetown, Barbados, to rendezvous with the *Carnegie*. They wouldn't set foot on mainland USA for ten months.

As a parting gift Norman gave Barbara an anchor pin for emotional and philosophical support. The *Frederick H.*'s ghostly anchor had been an important symbol for Barbara, and she sometimes drew one on her letters to Norman. Barbara's anchor included the three elements that, combined, represented her new philosophy, which she felt she needed following her father's departure. There's a lot of philosophical ruminating in her letters to Norman in 1928 and 1929, much of it transcribed in *Barbara Newhall Follett: A Life in Letters* (Farksolia, 2015).

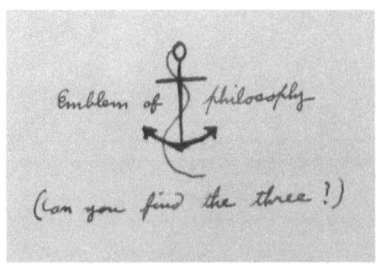

With Barbara's invaluable but uncredited help, Helen published two books about their adventures at sea: *Magic Port-*

holes (Macmillan, New York, 1932), which covered the West Indies, and *Stars to Steer By* (Macmillan, New York, 1934), which covered the rest.

As for Barbara, sailing away from home that September launched the second half of her all-too-brief life and provided material for her final novel, the terrific *Lost Island* (Farksolia, 2020). Or was Barbara's in fact an all-too-brief life? I think the remains that were found in 1948 on Pulsifer Hill near Plymouth, New Hampshire — half a mile from the house she and her husband rented for winter getaways — were Barbara's remains, but I will probably never know for sure. According to New Hampshire authorities the remains are lost. The mystery of Barbara, however, is intact.

> She was a fairy — a wood nymph. She would be invisible for ever to all mortals, save those few who have minds to believe, eyes to see. To these she is ever present, the spirit of Nature — a sprite of the meadow, a naiad of lakes, a nymph of the woods.
>
> — Barbara Newhall Follett, *The House Without Windows*, 1927

Notes on a Junior Author
(with a glance at precocity)
Wilson Follett

THE EDITOR of *The Horn Book* has asked me for some informal jottings on the young author of *The House Without Windows* (1927) and *The Voyage of the Norman D.* (1928), in spite of a pair of the most complete disqualifications ever heard of. I am, to begin with, one-half of all the parents this author owns; and I am, to go on with, an active part of the only publishing establishment with which she has ever had a connection. If a father could contemplate with an outsider's detachment the work of his own child, it would be pretty remarkable. If a publisher could judge as a disinterested critic the items of his own list, out of which he makes (or tries to make) his living, it would also be a fairly noteworthy occurrence. And if the two things were to happen together, I am afraid we should have to view the combined result as being off the ground of ordinary events and somewhere up in the domain of sheer miracle.

The only thing I can do is turn my cards face up and let the reader make his own allowances in his own way. Frankly, then, speaking as a person and a parent, I like this Barbara Newhall Follett very much indeed, with an esteem which extends to her writings; and, speaking as a publisher, I expect her two books to live for a good while, making their way in the world with unobtrusive success, and to be added to from time to time as the author's engagements and the customs of publishing make convenient.

* * *

When an adolescent writes a book, every one murmurs the word "precocity." If the word isn't murmured, it is shouted or shrieked. This response has nothing to do with the intrinsic qualities of the book, or with the qualities of mind and personality embodied in the book: the chorus starts up as soon as the book is announced for publication, and it is based on nothing whatever except that twelve and thirteen-year-olds are not commonly authoring for fun, because that isn't commonly their idea of fun.

I shall have this to say of any charge of precocity, as applied to the twelve-year-old author of *The House Without Windows* and the thirteen-year-old author of *The Voyage of the Norman D.*: To anybody who wants to be rational enough to entertain for a moment the thought that the measure of a workman is his work, the following idea will probably make sense: namely, that a book is precocious or not according to whether the mental traits and perceptions expressed in it are or are not in advance of the author's chronological age at the time of writing it. A fundamental diagnosis of Barbara's case is this: She is, at fourteen, an eleven-year-old, as childhood's interests go. If she were fifteen, instead of fourteen, one would have to call her an instance of arrested development.

* * *

Notes on a Junior Author

Everything works together to drive children into premature imitation of adult interests. The system gets them going and coming. Childhood is made intolerable by condescending books, plays, pictures, and games, all invented out of whole cloth by "educational psychologists" whose theories of the child-mind are invented out of the same whole cloth; and all the most inane, trivial, and tawdry aspects of grown-up life are ready to hand for the child's models of ambition and behavior. First, we take out of childhood all that makes it comfortable for children; and then we fill up the void with the offscourings of our own existence — the fashions of wasting time which we know aren't even good enough for *us*, and which sour to even our own vitiated taste in the very hours of our pretended enjoyment. Precocity, which is always imitation, would not be so poisonous if there were anything in sight worth imitating.

There are certain realities which ought to be part of every child's inalienable inheritance, and of which we systematically disinherit nearly all children. The chief of such important realities are, perhaps, these: (1) leisure; (2) privacy when required; (3) freedom; (4) familiarity with nature; (5) spontaneous activity; (6) gratification of curiosity; (7) equal companionship when needed; (8) the right to be taken seriously as a human being at all times. There is no room here to define these *seriatim* or to diagram the ways in which on each count we contrive to rob children of their due. Suffice it to say that the completely *normal* child is one who has had the fullest measure of this inheritance that is humanly possible. And the *average* child of twelve or fourteen — so well do our civilized machinations prosper — is one who has been as completely deprived of all eight of these natural advantages as the insane ingenuity of the race can manage. The result is that childish normality has all but disappeared from urban America. We habitually construe a warped and malformed *average* as the norm.

Wilson Follett

It is my present notion that Barbara Newhall Follett is an example of the norm of childhood, undevastated by the average perversion. She has a normal set of interests instead of a precociously imitative set (and is therefore regarded as underdeveloped); and she has a normally articulate power of expression instead of the usual speech-bound paralysis (and is therefore regarded as overdeveloped). In both particulars she reaps the advantage and pays the penalty of not having been fussed at and tampered with — of having been let alone.

* * *

She has been let alone. She has had her own room from birth, her own study and collection of books from the age of reading. She has chosen her books, has read what she could get pleasure out of, and has reread things as often or as seldom as she chose. She has never been herded in gangs, or standardized into any sort of pattern. She has never entered a school except for a few minutes as a visitor. She has run wild in the country for months at a time, learning birds, animals, insects, trees, ferns, flowers. She has climbed mountains of altitudes suited to her age, and carried packs graduated to her strength. She has swung a paddle, and swum like a young water-rat, and sailed a rude makeshift contraption in wild weather, and slept on the ground, and pawed mountain cranberries from under snow with numbed fingers, and tamed deer mice. Out of pure curiosity, she has used a typewriter haltingly at four, accurately at five, fluently at six, with professional competence at seven, until at eight the expression of her thoughts through its keys was nearly as instinctive as breathing. She has asked questions and got them answered — when there were answers that could be found. She has had a perennial crop of overlapping grand passions (Anglicè, "crushes") — two year's absorption in clocks; five in a particular stuffed animal; three in butterflies; in Ludwig von Beethoven; in ships and the sea; in yellow as a color; in the Roman tongue and Julius Caesar personally; in pirates and piracy — and no one has sat on them or laughed at them. She has picked up a business-like habit of finishing what she starts, along with a wildly adventurous habit of starting whatever comes into her head. And, enviably, she has laughed more in her fourteen years than I have in my forty.

Now, it is my belief and contention that all this is natural, normal; and that her two books (which are nothing if not an embodiment of it) are expressions of the normal, natural child. Every one seems to have agreed that they are — at any rate in English — the only books of their kind. The reason for that is not that she is a paragon or a freak; it is that she is about the only articulate fourteen-year-old in America whom nobody has ever tried to pour into a preconceived mold. Her writing is composed of just the sunlight that would saturate *any* child's consciousness if we could only make up our minds to give nature half a chance. She is exceptional simply in her unhindered retention to the age of fourteen of interests which we ridicule and thrash and educate out of most children at nine or ten. Barbara is, I think and hope, an individual in the literary use she makes of her interests. But those interests themselves are the natural and characteristic property of every child on earth that has been given decent surroundings, decent companionship, *and* a decent letting alone.

All of this must sound as if I considered Barbara a perfect being and a paragon — which is the opposite of what I am trying to say. She is normal childhood; and she has, of course, her defects as all of us do. I have ideas about some of the defects; but this is not a paper on that subject. It is written not to pick a personality to pieces, but to summarize the causative forces that made Barbara's two books an entirely natural form of expression.

In fine, the books exist because they were allowed to; because she was allowed to be the way she is. No one tried to stop her. When she wanted to typewrite, no one said, "Oh no, you have to learn to write first," or "Oh, no, you have to learn to read first," or "Oh no, you aren't going to be a stenographer," or "Oh no, the motions of typewriting are against the laws of eurythmy." When she wanted to write a story (*The House Without Windows*) to give to her mother on her own ninth birthday, no one said, "Oh no, you don't *give* things on your birthday; you *get* them." The usual devices for the destruction of initiative and curiosity were not applied to her at all. Pains were taken with her upbringing — pains to stand out of her sunlight, to give her air, to let her go it [sic].

It is implicit in all the foregoing that Barbara is indebted to the universe principally for a mother who had convictions, and, in consistent daily practice over a term of years, the courage of them. Lots of mothers will agree thoroughly, in discussion, with the principle of the thing — which, indeed, is like many another precept of elementary horse-sense that everybody accepts and nobody applies. But Barbara had the improbable luck to draw a mother who didn't take it all out in talk. She supplied, out of her own abundance, what the child demanded. That was important. And she spared, with unremitting self-restraint, what the child didn't demand. That was perhaps even more important. Maternity is usually construed — by its practitioners — as a commission to adapt the child to a preconceived society (either the mother's own kind of society or a kind that she has missed and doesn't mean to let her child miss). Barbara Follett's mother took maternity, rather, as a chance to find out what was in the child and let it come out. She had the originality to think the job through, the mental and personal resources to do the job day by day in the thick of great material difficulties, and the aplomb to send all interferences (and interferers) politely to the devil.

Personally, I am convinced that the world is more in her debt than the world is likely to know or admit; first, for a heterodox and very courageous experiment in education; secondly, for the preservation, unspoiled and unpampered, of the subject of her experiment, who looks to me to be worth something to the world by virtue of her differences; thirdly, and more tangibly, for the two books which she allowed to write themselves — the one a fundamental revelation of the very soul of natural childhood, the second an eager acceptance of as beautiful an adventure as is possible to childhood. But I shall not quarrel with any one who charges these opinions of mine to inevitable prejudice, or disagrees with them on every count. We are all fond of our own ways of thinking, and reasoning about them is only our technique for discovering *ex post facto* the rational justification of beliefs that we can no more help than we can help the color of our eyes.

The Voyage of the Norman D. and *The House Without Windows* stand or fall, ultimately, by the amount of delight they are able to give; and this, after all, is a question of fact and experience. It is not a question of theory, or of the author's age, or of what some one thinks about educational psychologists (a subject as extraneous to literature as to all other realities). If the books are good between title-page and finis, they will be no more and no less good if written by a committee of psychiatrists, or by the Beef Trust, or by a Ouija board. The proof of the author is in the book; and the proof of the book is in the reading.

Barbara's document in code

Item (5) in "Note from the Publisher": *The endpapers consist of a document in code with which the author amused herself during one interval in the composition of the letter.*

Barbara's document in code

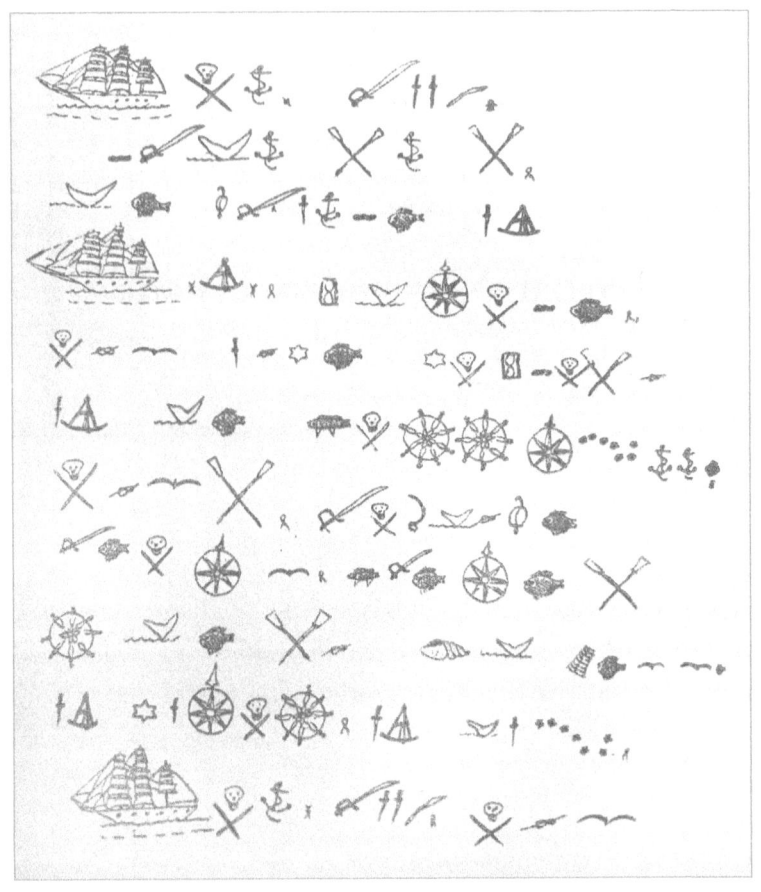

Barbara's document in code

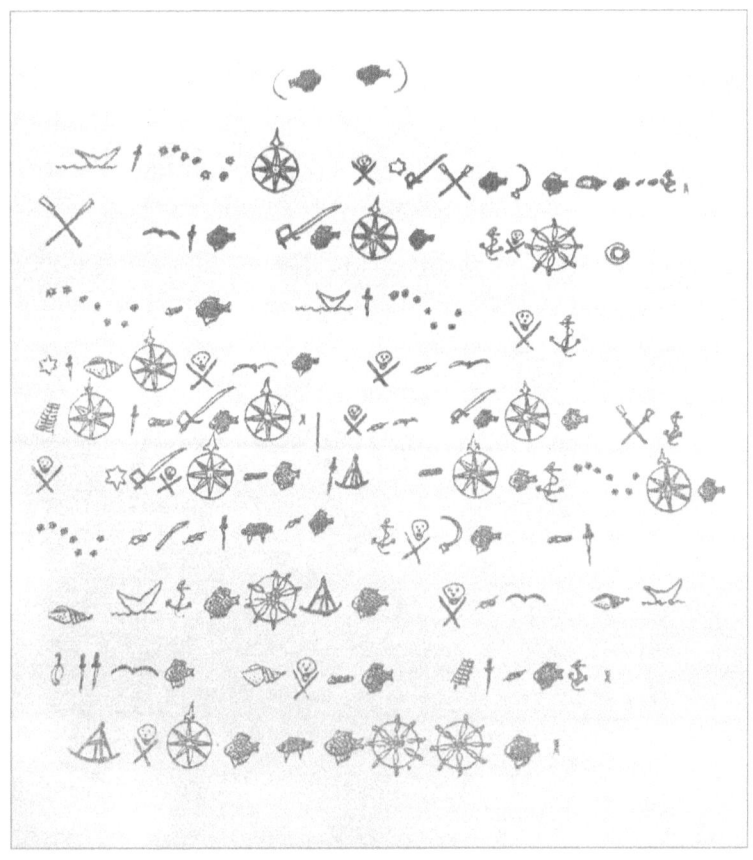

Notes

The Voyage of the Norman D.

1. The cook's pronunciation; I have not found the word as yet. The process is lowering buckets for sea water and washing down the deck.
2. The beginning of what Roy called "The Rosewood Casket," as he played and whistled it.

www.ingramcontent.com/pod-product-compliance
Lightning Source LLC
Chambersburg PA
CBHW030434010526
44118CB00011B/632